T5-CVQ-069

HOMOSEXUALS ANONYMOUS

A Psychoanalytic & Theological Analysis of Colin Cook & His Cure for Homosexuality

Arthur Frederick Ide

Garland
Tangelwüld Press
1987

Published by
Tangelwüld Press
Garland, Texas

BR
115
.H6
I 33
1987

©1987, Arthur Frederick Ide

Library of Congress Cataloging-in-Publication Data

Ide, Arthur Frederick
 Homosexuals anonymous.

 Includes bibliography and index.
 1. Homosexuality--Religious aspects--Christianity--
Controversial literature.   2. Cook, Colin.   I. Title.
BR115.H6I33   1987   261.8'35766   87-6487
ISBN 0-934667-06-3 (pbk.)

For

Brett Allan Pyles-Baker

Ἡδέως μὲν ἔχε πρὸς ἅπαντας, χρῶ δὲ τοῖς βελτίστοις. -Isocrates.

Scott R. Buttram

Αὔξεται δ' ἀρετά, χλωραῖς ἐέρσαις ὡς ὅτε δένδρον ἀΐσσει. -Pindar.

and

Jere Hinckley

Πολλῷ τὸ φρονεῖν εὐδαιμονίας πρῶτον ὑπάρχει. -Sophocles.

"Be gracious to all men, but choose the best to be your friends."

Isocrates

"Noble deeds grow before the eyes of men, even as a tree waxes great when watered by the quickening dew.

Pindar

"Wisdom is the most important part of happiness."

Sophocles

TABLE OF CONTENTS

Foreword

Unmasking Hypocrisy

by J. Michael Clark, M.Div., Ph.D.
Emory University

Building upon a number of his previous studies
of gay people and homophobia, particularly the recent *Gomorrah and the Rise of Homophobia* (The
Liberal Press, 1985), Arthur Frederick Ide fuses
powerful gay-sensitive emotions with in-depth
scholarship in the present volume, in order to unmask
the misinformed psychological and theological tenets,
the misguided cruelty, and the basic hypocrisy under-
girding one specific program to "convert" or "cure"
homosexuals—that of Colin Cook. This volume clearly functions on two levels. The general, gay-sensitive
reader will be intrigued and dismayed by Dr. Ide's
forty pages of primary text; scholarly readers will be
stimulated by some thirty-seven pages of thorough-
going citation and explanatory notes.

Moving from a basic introduction to the fundamental principles of psychoanalysis, Ide describes the
manner in which right wing theology co-opts psychology and how that dubious mix can be homophob-
ically exploited against vulnerable gay people. In this
context, he examines Colin Cook and his Quest
Learning Center's program for gay people. Briefly an
ordained Seventh Day Adventist minister, Cook trans-
formed his own very particular, personal autobio-
graphy—his own unsuccessful struggle with homosexuality and his deep entrenchment in fundamentalist
religious dogma—into a "universal" norm to shape his
"therapeutic" program, a plan which further anach-
ronistically retained the causality-oriented and misinformed anti-gay psychological dogma of the 1950s
and 1960s (prior to the declassification of homosex-

uality as a mental illness). He further labelled the existential standpoint of being gay, "atheistic," in direct opposition to Carl Jung's earlier assessment that gay men, in particular, exhibit an enhanced spiritual capacity. The mixture of Cook's therapeutic norm with utterly unsupportable biblical exegesis produced the "H Solution," the very name of which links his program to another "solution" which took nearly a quarter million gay lives between 1936 and 1945 under Nazism. If for no other reason, the implied warning in Ide's text of the extreme danger of fundamentalist "cures" for homosexuality makes this work of value to a gay community increasingly embattled by a now AIDS-related homophobia.

With no small amount of sardonic humor, Ide proceeds beyond his analysis of the psychological and theological motivations of Cook's program. He also carefully documents the scandal surrounding Cook's own 1986 admission that he had sexually manipulated and abused his male clients. The "repentent" and now married and familied Cook's own homosexuality further undercut his already unworkable "cure." Ide reveals that "none of the 'counselees' at Quest changed his sexual orientation—and no one knew of anyone who had"; moreover, Cook was unable to cure himself!

Overall, then, Ide's small yet powerful monograph fuses heart-felt emotions and scholarly research to warn the gay community of the danger and hypocrisy involved in all fundamentalist homophobia and anti-gay efforts, through one vividly portrayed "case study." It is a case study with which all gay-supportive persons should become familiar.

Atlanta, Georgia
March 1987

HOMOSEXUALS ANONYMOUS

Arthur Frederick Ide

Arthur Frederick Ide

Introduction

The pristine purpose of psychology is to understand the human mind. This classic definition is adjunct to psychoanalysis which has the purpose of investigating the subconscious. The wedding of psychology and psychoanalysis has resulted in the genesis of psychotherapy that is based on the theory that mental symptoms express socially forbidden desires which are not consciously acknowledged. Early works in psychotherapy, such as those by Austrian Sigmund Freud (1856-1939), were attempts ("treatments") to bring pathogenic (deeply repressed) motives and memories to the surface with the help of dream interpretation and free association.

Freud's thesis is that all adult adjustments and maladjustments spring from the Oedipus complex, whereby the child is sexually drawn to the parent of the opposite sex and jealous of the other parent. In explanation of this theory, Freud declared that sex is one of the key forces in all of human life. At the same time sex is a major facet in the history of human life and interchange. Sex, at is basic, is propelled and develops through the *libido*. The *libido* is the most primitive stage of sex. The *libido* moves human beings towards living. If the *libido* is restricted, living becomes painful, repressive, uneventful, and sometimes generates *thanatos*—or a psychological and/or physical movement toward death.

Personality is developed around the *id* The *id* operates on a "pleasure principle," and as such is *socially irrational* in communities where personal pleasure is subordinate to group pleasure. Societial laws and customs regulate the *id* through the *ego* (basic reason), and ultimately through control of the *superego* (conscience) which is indoctrinated from birth by familial, peer and community (religious, social, economic, national, ethnic, etc.) standards that bring about, voluntarily or involuntarily, social acceptance and practice. Such uniformity, however, is not always good for the individual or the individual psychology (*psyche*).

Originally psychology, psychoanalysis and psychotherapy was heralded as a way for individuals who were not in step with society to find a way to follow the dictates of that society. For more than fifty years social psychologists were busy at reprogramming non-conformists to fit the socially acceptable model. When such therapy led to a self-realization and self-acceptance of the self in tune with society both society and the patient benefited. However, with the advent of the 1940s—carried through the 1970s—psychology labored feverishly to transmorgify primary personal means of expression that had little to do with the individual's social interaction. Not only was the overt social actions of a social non-conformist to be changed, but too, the personal sexual preference of the individual was to be enchained by a primitive pastoral code of ontological/theological theory that rudimentarily and teleologically trumpeted tribal customs and history of a limited number of people who lived nomadically on the rugged hills of the Middle East: the Holiness Code of the ancient Hebrews who damned all non-Hebrew people as being idolators and rejected their lifestyles and expressions of worship—many of which included sexual acts of devotion. This was especially true if those sexual acts of worship included same-gender coupling and sexual orgasmic release of seminal fluids.

With the rise of Hebrew/Jewish/Christian thought and its acceptance/enforcement on/by the wider Roman empire, the same phobiae of the ancient Hebrews became the letter of the law of rural areas and the emerging churches—few of which understood the pagan antecedents that actually generated the restrictions to full expression of self-actualization and development. Theology became psychology and

and law to the detriment of individual psychology
and happiness, especially when the Christian church
took a stand against homosexuality by wrongly and
unscientifically terming it "unnatural," even though
the ancients and even some early Christian thinkers
detailed its existence and practice in the world of
nature.[1]

Although many priests and nuns were gay in
the evolving church, the gynophobes/homophobes/
sexual-phobes,[2] carried the day because of position
and power bestowed upon them by a weak local ruler
who saw the church as a controllable force to be ex-
erted over the masses.[3] The sexual phobiae of the
church became law and ruined numerous lives with
some religious adherents disappearing into the woods
or deserts, others renouncing their embryonic faiths,
while the majority caved in under the pressure and
accepted passively the enchainment of their own pre-
ferences and proclivities to a rigid format in exchange
for an opportunity to live in familiar surroundings
and with their family, friends, and community.

The bastardization and transmorgification of
human will and ultimately of individual psychology
pushed on with little abatement until the late 1970s.
"Treatment" of homosexuality has been the *raison
d'etre* of generations of homophobes mascarading as
theologians and psychologists—all determined to
stiffle if not change that orientation which they have
been personally uncomfortable around—even if that
interest had never been directed toward them.[4] In
many cases, as found in the writings of Elizabeth
Moberly,[5] psychology has been taken over and trans-
formed into a vehicle for theology,[6] with no thought
for the welfare or ultimate self-actualization of the
patient, but instead only the growth of church/eccles-
iological confessors and church goers who could fund
an already engorged treasury.

This book looks closely at one of the greatest
Christian charades of compassion and "cure" for

homosexuality in the late twentieth century. Misusing scriptural citations to support personal phobiae, Colin Cook developed an organization for his self-interests and personal needs which ultimately led him to abuse the very clientele he had promised to cure. His lectures against homosexuality, which were studded with biblical quotations, were applauded by such "distinguished" practioneers as Dr. William P. Wilson, Professor Emeritus of the Department of Psychiatry, Duke University Medical Center, who declared that he was "impressed" with Cook's "Biblical base...[and] his psychological soundness," and Dr. Richard F. Lovelace, Professor of Church History at Gordon-Conwell Seminary, who declared "In listening to Cook I knew I was listening to original and fine theology with a lucidity and personal voice of its own."[7]

Christian love and charity has been turned to homophobic hating by the pillars of organized fundamentalist churches who fear that which they do not understand, avoid that which does not threaten them, and condemn that which has never judged their actions, interests or proclivities. While there is a companion volume on the "cure" of homosexuality to appear soon, this volume addresses primary Christian hypocrisy as expressed and lived by Colin Cook and his Quest Learning Center in Reading, Pennsylvania.

—Arthur Frederick Ide

20 February 1987

NOTES

[1] Και ει θηλειαι αλληλας αναβαινουσιν οταν της προς αρρενα μιξεως ατυχησωσι, Aelian Varia historia 1:15; cp. Plutarch, De sollertia animalium in Moralia 972D-F. It is interesting to note that those Christian theologians who wrote condemning homosexuality also wrote at length condemning heterosexuality; see my Woman as Priest, Bishop & Laity, chapt. 6, and Augustine of Hippo, Contra mendacium 17:34, in J.-P. Migne, Patrologia...ser. Latina 40:542. Augustine notes that homosexuality was not so rare as he thought in his exclamation "Quae si omnes gentes facerent, eodem." Augustine had a difficult time in accepting sex, and was known to repudiate his own comments on sex depending on time, place, reason or condition (see his De bono conjugali 16:18 (PL, 40:385) where he affirms it, and then repudiates it in Retractiones 22: 2; cf. Contra Julianum 4.14.67 (PL, 44:771).) His condemnation of homosexuality is based on its "infamiliarity" with him and his belief that homosexuality is the result of desire for carnal knowledge and lust (Confessions 3.8 (PL, 32:689-90), for he was not aware that homosexuals do love and make commitments, with many gay couples in the fifth century actually marrying and living their lives together while on earth (see my Gomorrah & the Rise of Homophobia, pp. 29, 36; cf. John Boswell, Christianity, Social Tolerance and Homosexuality, pp. 26ff.).

[2] Peter the Venerable, De miraculis 1.14 (PL, 189:878), Peter Cantor, De vitio sodomitico (PL, 205:333-335), Pope Honorius III Epistle to Archbishop of Lund, in Bullarium Danicum, ed. A. Krarup (Copenhagen, 1932), no. 208, and Peter Damian, Liber Gomorrhianus which blasts homosexuality among the clergy. See my Homosexuality and the Clergy, chap. 5.

[3] Charlemagne was an exception in strength, however his alleged statute(s) against homosexuality have been proven to be forgeries by Benedict of Levita. See F.L. Ganshof, Recherches sur les capitulaires (Paris, 1958), p. 71f.

[4] Quest. "Homosexuality and the Church," pamphlet, p. [4].

[5] Cf. her Homosexuality: A New Christian Ethic (Stony Point, SC).

[6] Quest, loc. cit.

[7] Ibid.

Chapter One

Colin Cook

Colin Cook was born in England. The British
Isles were at war with Nazi Germany. The United
States had not yet entered World War II, although
most Americans believed it would be but a matter of
time until the Giant in the West moved against Japan.
Men were at a premium in England during the
war years. Men were to be warriors. They were to be
trained to kill. They were not to shed, share, or express emotion. "A stiff upper-lip" was the rule. Any
other sign of emotion was not only effeminine, but
tantamount to cowardice. Colin Cook was born into
this environment.

Outside of the memories and notes scribbled
by a later Colin, there is little record of Cook's father.
What is known is that the senior Cook was a fisher-
man. What can be inferred is that the father had little
time for "women's needs": tenderness, religion or
faith. After 1978, Colin wrote that he was not "led to
faith in Christ" until he had attained the age of 15.[1]

Colin's love for Christ was built upon a strict,
biblical literalism fostered by a conservative fundamentalism that was to permeate his life and leave its
indelible mark upon his psychology. What the King
James Version of the Christian Protestant Bible said
was bad—was bad. Colin was taught not to question.
He elected to stand in awed terror of the wrathful
God of Moses, the unrelenting theology of Paul, and
the distortions of ancient scrolls by seventeenth
century divines that had clustered at Hampton Court
at the instance of King James VI & I who dabbled
in theology when he was not busy courting the amor-
ous adventures and attention of his favorite courtier—
George Villiers ("Stinky"), the Duke of Buckingham

(who was seldom hesitant to use his "prowess in the royal bed" when he sought a special boon, adventure, rank, or advance into a "glory" or position).[2] The fact that even though the King James Version is resoundingly elegant and dramatic prose it does not enjoy the same high marks for factuality and scholarship as a careful and actual presentation of the exact wording of the ancient scrolls on which it is allegedly based; yet this has made no difference to Colin at any point in his life of less than fifty years.[3]

Colin was a strict conservative. His life revolved around the concept that he should not lay up treasures on earth for he might not find treasures in the life to come. Denial was considered a glory if it was personal denial "for the love of Jesus." Enchained to this ideological opiate, willingly accepting the yoke of ecclesiological and christological commandments that he surrender his personality for the love of a vengeful God, Cook the Younger left home and entered a seminary. Once more his life was flooded with religious literature, learning, deprivation, self-denial and self-condemnation. The metaphysical sack cloth and ashes that he adorned himself with finally paid off, when, at twenty-five he was ordained a minister of the homophobic Seventh Day Adventist Church.[4]

The accounts differ. Some record that Colin maintained his ministerial position for seven years.[5] Others argue that he was a clergyman in practice for nine years.[6] Regardless, it was during this time that Colin wore the clerical markings of a "man of God" he recognized his own homosexuality.[7]

Being a homosexual was painful for Colin. It defied everything he had been taught to believe in: that homosexuality was biblically wrong, that sex outside of marriage was evil, and that heaven was closed to those who did not engage in supine sexuality for the sake of procreation. The torment was unbearable.

Realizing that he was a homosexual, and confessing that he was "fully under an addiction to homosexuality" by 1971, at least three years before he left the Seventh Day Adventist ministry, Colin Cook entered the Underworld Culture of gay men and women—a marginalized minority of human beings that has been outcast by the crass ignorance of a society that is shackled to the tales of yesteryear, the fantasies of fanatics, and the terrors of traditionalists who cloak their private ambitions behind horatory holy screens of myths, allegories, and inaccuracies.[8]

For at least seven years Colin Cook suffered under his own mind paralysis: unwilling to allow himself to celebrate the reality of his own existence as a worthwhile being in tune with nature, discounting his own basic goodness as a natural phenomenon ordained to develop his destiny by his own impulses, power, predelicitions and penchant, to cave instead into an antiquated misreading and transmorgification of ancient documents that stole from him his dignity, humanity, and quality. To end this torture he accupunctured his personal spirit, denied himself and his own importance, put aside self-actualization and self-acceptance and confused himself into a heterosexist mentality. Blistering with self-condemnation for being real and living one of many forms of natural lifestyles, Cook sought escape from himself through the traditional door of a heterosexual marriage.

In 1978 Cook took a wife.[9] By Sharon he realized his biological ability to generate a living fetus that evolved into the person of Christopher. This, he was convinced, was a sign that his god ordained coitus as the "only" means of sexual expression and its ultimate purpose: procreation—even though not every seed he sewed inside his socially acceptable wife fertilized one of her eggs, nor attached itself to the uterus, nor generated to a developing embryo. Christopher was but an accident—but that could not be admitted for it would tend to tear the Christian message apart before the truths of science and generation.

Colin Cook's marriage and subsequent father-hood gave him a "new birth." In the manner of near-ly all converts to a cause or principle, Colin became a zealot attacking not only himself, what he had been, what he had experienced, but also the people that occupied the same Underworld he rejected when he could no longer handle the dichotomy raging in his mind in conflict between actual experience and theological propagandic indoctrination and mind control. But as much as he spoke against homosexu-ality, he could not escape the fact that he had only "subdued" his own gay feelings—not changed them.[10]

In addressing the issue of homosexuality and public recognition and/or tolerance/acceptance of the gay life style—an option in the realm of nature that is open not only to birds[11] but also to mammals on various planes and plateaus[12] in the evolutionary process of species maturational development—Colin attempts to argue, without professional competence, training, recognition or sanction, that homosexuality is the result of a "state of emotional deficit." He claims that homosexuals seek love from "members of their own sex in an effort to make up for a lack of love from their parents of the same sex."[13] He bases his hypothesis and conclusions not on any scientific or clinical study, but instead upon his own personal experience with his father who was "away from home for long periods of time."[14] His father's absence made Colin feel rejected, hurt, unwanted, unloved, and, by analogy from his public pontifications on various college campuses where he has spoken, he stopped identifying with the father he hardly knew and sought a surrogate or substitute father by turning to other men for a love he had not experienced. Uniquely this love was one which was sexual—a love that his own father more than likely would never have given him, nor which his own ontological confessiology would have entoned, affirmed, or sanctified.

Once Colin Cook articulates his hypothesis on homosexuality being generated by an indifferent and unloving parent, counselors frequently on the same campus where the lecture was given rise to voice professional skepticism. Lorraine Curte of Grand Rapids, Michigan, commented that Cook's views on the causes of homosexuality were dubious and too general, for while some homosexuals did have childhoods similar to the ones that Cook described, many did not.[15]

In preaching his message of biblical distortion and untruths, Colin Cook has been buttressed by other "reformed homosexuals." Daniel Roberts, the Director of Communications at Cook's Quest Learning Center located in Reading, Pennsylvania, has taken especial pains to paint homosexuality as a selfish motif spawned by evil in an attempt to suppress "the truth about God." Homosexuality, it is alleged, is a form of atheism[16] or a "defensive detachment extended to the spiritual realm."[17] The longer that homosexuality is allowed to surface, express itself, propagate its "errors" by encouraging others to be or "remain" gay, the longer is "the truth about God" held down and the harder it is for any mortal to "know about himself." Roberts has written, "The genital and romantic intimacy one looks for in homosexuality is a symbolic confusion for the true intimacy which can be found only in the forgiveness, acceptance and love of God and its extension in godly [heterosexual] human relations."[18]

Without foundation in fact or based on any plausible study, Roberts has increased his attacks on Christian homosexuals by claiming that homosexuality is a "limitation of the individual's personality and identity." Yet conversion to the staid and ossified lifestyle that Cook and Roberts hold out as a balm in their Gilead is not easy, for "recovery" from homosexuality involves such factors as "the person's age, degree of involvement in homosexual activity and lifestyle, social skills, and quality of available [fundamentalist] Christian fellowship."[19]

Roberts' and Cook's god is extremely narrow, limiting, and self-defensive. In an attempt to defend this god and to support the deity's need to limit and control people like robots who are void of free will and personal conduct decisions, Roberts and Cook attack those churches that accept homosexuals for being the good people that most are. While reciting a message of "Christian love and forgiveness," Cook's group, Quest, soundly blast administrators of churches which hold conferences on homophobia. Cook demands that when there are conferences on gay life and lifestyles, the "conference" should be geared towards prayer for the homosexual, not a logical, thoughtful attempt to understand the homosexual and celebrate the homosexual's freedom to be the best person possible.[20]

Quick to pull the mote out of their brother's eye, and seldom willing to accept the beam in their own tunneled vision, Cook and Roberts, like the entire gaggle of spiritual geese that parade around the Quest Learning Center delight in noting how frequently their name is in print.[21] When trained professionals come out in opposition to the nefarious pronouncements of Cook and his gang, Quest stands defensive.[22] When 270 "concerned homosexuals" appear at an anti-gay seminar, the number is lauded as a "crowd;" yet when an equal or greater number of gays appear to participate in a meeting of the Universal Fellowship of Metropolitan Community Churches (most of whose members are gay, and a majority of its clergy from Pentacostal and other Christian fundamentalist groups) they are looked upon as an "insignificant group." [23] Testimonials for the "H Solution" ["converting" homosexuals into obedient Christian fundamentalist heterosexuals] come from anonymous ministers of all faiths, with glowing affirmations printed elegantly on the back of propaganda issued by Cook—always without a signature or address of the laudator.[24] Newsletters and other media complete the confusion.

A library is set up at the Quest Center. Cook has urged all members of his sect to gain as much news space as possible, and then admonished those who did capture news space to send clippings on Homosexuals Anonymous to him.[25] And then there is the factor of money.

Like most televangelists who follow in the footsteps of greed walked by Tammy and Jim Bakker who rake in millions of untaxed dollars per year, or Oral Roberts who extorts money from his followers lest god take his life if he does not raise $4.5 million, or Pat Robertson whose engorged coffers have built a university (CBN), radio and television station, and other propaganda tools, Cook also wants to cash in on the biggest contemporary sham confidence game in twentieth century America: milking millions for Jesus.[26] The *Homosexuals Anonymous Fellowship Services Policy and Advisory Manual* has been revised to "suggest that 10% of your weekly collections be sent to HAFS. ... No large funds should accumulate at the local chapter level."[27] Although this is policy, Cook has taken pains to address it by writing in the April 1986 *HA News* that "We are not demanding this contribution of you. ... We hope rather that the relationship of HAFS and the local chapters will be one of love and respect for what we have to offer you."[28]

To get "input" and to offer "counsel," Cook has acquired a toll-free number as "a permanent fixture."[29] He has written a book (*Homosexuality: An Open Door?*) whose royalties he plows back into his organization.[30] The book feeds on fear.

8

NOTES

[1] Homosexuals Anonymous Fellowship Services, "Homosexuality and the Church: A Ministry of Healing." [HAFS pamphlet (Reading, PA: HAFS, 1986), p. 2]

[2] Henry Ellis (ed.), *Original Letters Illustrative of English History* (London, 1825; 1st ser. 3 vols.) III:119 offers insight into James' idolization for Buckingham whose health and wellbeing meant more to him than many matters of State. Since James VI & I was far older than Buckingham he encouraged his son and heir to take Buckingham into his confidence and turn to him when he should inherit the throne. An interesting history on this colorful individual is by David Harris Willson, *King James VI & I* (New York: Oxford University Paperback, 1956, 1967), especially chapters 21-22. On James VI & I interference in religion, the commissioning of Hampton Court to render the Bible into "the King's English," see Roland G. Usher, *The Reconstruction of the English Church* (New York, 1910. 2 vols.) I:292-309, 316, the basic William Barlow, *The Summe and Substance of the Conference ...at Hampton Court* (1604), reprinted, with other material of the conference, in Edward Cardwell, *History of Conferences* (Oxford, 1840). The KJV was created to insure conformity of religious thinking in England not to strengthen the faith but to unify the nation (the Bishop's Bible was the official bible of the Anglican church, while the people used the Geneva Bible most commonly, which James considered the worst of all). In this regard James required the conference translators to follow the Bishop's Bible as far as possible, which meant that words which had several meanings had to be translated according to the venial and corrupt interpretations of the early Church fathers and not according to understood interpretation. Cf. James Craigie (ed.), *The Basilikon Doron of King James VI* (Scottish Text Society, 3rd. ser., nos. 16, 18. Edinburgh, 1944, 195. 2 vols.) I:37, II:93; and, David Daiches, *The King James Version of the English Bible* (Chicago, 1941), 63-72, 155-171. See also my *Myths, Mistakes and Errors in the Christian Bible* (Chicago, 1978).

[3] "Hope for the Homosexual," *Charisma* (May 1984), 61. Douglas McIntyre, "Homosexuality: A Bridge Crossed," (Reading, PA: HAFS, n.d.; cassette tape).

[4] George Berkin, "Homosexuals learn power of faith," (Reading, PA) *Eagle/Times* (15 September 1981), Colin took

a master's degree in religion and New Testament theology from Andrews University (Seventh Day Adventist), in Berrien Springs, Michigan. His education permeates his thinking and writing—along strict literal reading of English transmorgifications of the Christian Protestant bible.

[5] Berkin, *ibid.*, states "nine years," while the HAFS flier "Homosexuality and the Church" (p. [2]) gives seven. Interestingly Berkin's article is not certain that Cook is truly "converted" from homosexuality. He writes: "Six years afterward [since Cook left the ministry] Cook *feels* he is now fully free" (emphasis mine)—he does not state that Cook *knows* that he is free. This is in line with contemporary thought, a reality expressed by most members of the American Psychiatric Association and American Psychological Association that homosexuality is not an optional facet in the psychological life of a man or woman, but is instead an intrinsic part of that life. Although Cook's belief in the "curability" of homosexuality was common through the 1960s, "curability" was never universally or fully accepted, with D. Stanley-Hones, "Sexual Inversion: the Problem of Treatment," *Medical Press* 218 (1947):212-215, arguing that the "true invert" [homosexual] gives society little to worry about, and "successful treatment" for him is questionable. J. Srnec and Kurt Freund, "Treatment of Male Homosexuality through Conditioning," *International Journal of Sexology* 7(2, 1953):92-93, reported that while 10 out of 25 homosexual patients were "treated" with a subcutaneous injection of a mixture of emetine, apomorphine, pilocarpine and ephedrine (which led the patients to vomit as a result of the mixture within 5-10 minutes), their "conversion" to heterosexuality was no more than a short-term shift of desire in a heterosexual direction. Alexander B. Smith and Alexander Bassin, "Group Therapy with Homosexuals," *Journal of Social Therapy* 5(3, 1959):225-232, acknowledge that peer pressure in group situations psychologically forced a homosexual to accept social conformity and "be" heterosexual—but only as long as the same social group was together. This was also the finding of M. Roman, "The Treatment of the Homosexual in the Group," *Topical Problems in Psychotherapy* 5(1965):170-175. A few years later psychologists and psyciatrists were beginning to accept the reality that homosexuality is neither a mental illness nor a disease but a psychological orientation, and that homosexual men and women would benefit the most from the professional who worked at helping the homosexual to accept and adjust to his or her situation; see E. Philipp, "Homosexuality as Seen in a New Zealand City Practice," *New Zealand Medical Journal* 67 (430, 1968):397-

401; and, Ronald Bayer, *Homosexuality and American Psychiatry: The Politics of Diagnosis* (New York: Basic Books, 1981). I shall discuss this at length later in this book.

[6] HAFS, *loc. cit.*.; cp. American Cassette Ministries, "Healing for the Homosexual," flier (Harrisburg: PA [1984?]. Most general publicity on Cook omits any reference; see The Grand Rapids, Michigan *Press*, (9 January 1986), C2; Calvin Bratt, "Metanoia Pushes Homosexuals Anonymous," [a photocopy sent to me by Cook]; Dawn M. Maurer, "Insight: A Hidden World" Reading, Pennsylvania *Eagle/Times* (23 October 1983) 1f; Liz O'Connor, "Approach to helping homosexuals presented at A.C.T. conference," *The Long Island* [New York] *Catholic* (23 May 1985), p. 2.

[7] Richard Lovelace, "New Resources for Homosexual Liberation," *Presbyterians United for Biblical Concerns* (Summer 1985), p. 7.

[8] J.R. Spangler and Colin Cook, "The H Solution," *Ministry* (September, 1981; reprinted as a pamphlet by Quest (Reading, PA, n.d.) in oversize format). 9 pgs. A counter to this giving celebration to gay ministry is J. Michael Clark, M.Div., Ph.D., *The Ganymede Papers: Essays in Gay Spirituality* (Garland, TX: Tangelwüld Press, 1987; distributed by Publishers Associates, Las Colinas, TX), and Maury Johnston, *Gays Under Grace: A Christian's Response to the Moral Majority* (Nashville, TN: Winston-Derek Publishers, 1983).

[9] HAFS, *loc. cit.*

[10] Susan Collins, *loc. cit.*

[11] Wainwright Churchill, *Homosexual Behavior among Males: A Cross-Cultural and Cross-Species Investigation* (New York, 1967). George Hunt and Molly Hunt, "Female-Female Pairing in Western Gulls (*Larus occidentalis*) in Southern California," *Science* 196 (1977):81-83. Homosexuality among animals has been known since the ancient Greeks, with lesbian activities among pigeons being recorded by Aelian, Plutarch, and others. See below.

[12] Cf. John Boswell, *Christianity, Social Tolerance and Homosexuality: Gay People in Western Europe from the Beginning of the Christian Era to the Fourteenth Century* (Chicago, 1980), pp. 303-334.

Cook rejects the work of Boswell on the ground that
Boswell is "a self-affirmed homosexual," and laments "many
frustrated homosexuals seeking peace and equilibrium have accepted [his] thinking, as well as many heterosexual individuals
who are sympathetic to their lifestyle." "The H Solution," p.
[2]. Cook rejects his thesis, and that of other authors who
have researched homosexuality on the grounds that they are
attempting to justify an "unacceptable" [to Christian fundamentalist thinking] lifestyle, a lifestyle he equates as being
close, if not tantamount, to alcoholism. This "disease" is not
to be "cured" unless the individual accept "the Gospel" (a
"fact" Cook laments will not come to pass quickly since
"within the heart of everyone of us lurks a hidden contempt
for the gospel", *ibid.*, p. [9]) which must be interpreted by
the individual according to strict literal standards affirmed by
Christian fundamentalists (*ibid.*, p. [11]). This acceptance,
which Cook bases on one line of Paul's *Letter to the Romans*
(1:17), however, has not been the ultimate and consuming
alkahest that he would wish, for at the same time Cook con-
fesses "that I still experience temptation from time to time
[to experience a homosexual encounter]" and therefore he
must struggle within himself to follow "When God calls"
down the path to psychosexual frustration, emotional un-
fullfillment, and personal deprivation (*loc. cit.*). It is a lonely
life filled with frustration.

[13]*Ibid.*, p. [2]. Maurer, *op. cit.*. Collins, *loc. cit.*.

[14]Collins, *ibid.*. Curte is a counselor who has worked
with gays in Grand Rapids for eighteen years. The idea that
homosexuality is the result of parental influence was rejected
as early as 1940 by Julius Bauer, "Homosexuality as an Endo-
crinological, Psychological, and Genetic Problem," *Journal of
Criminal Psychopathology* 2(2, 1940):188-197, who argued
that it "is caused" by abnormal chromosonal formation, and
that homosexuality may be hereditary. However, the study by
Roy A. Darke, "Hereditary as an Etiological Factor in Homosexuality," *Journal of Nervous and Mental Diseases* 107(Jan.-
June 1948):251-268, finds no evidence of an hereditary etiological determination of homosexuality in human beings.
Albert Ellis, "Constitutional Factors in Homosexuality: A Reexamination of the Evidence," in *Advances in Sex Research*,
ed. Hugo G. Beigel (New York, 1963), pp.161-186, adds that
most hypotheses that have been presented lack objective, con-
firmatory evidence of a scientific nature. The psychological
"findings" that Cook cites are equally spurious. Further discussion of this issue is given below.

[15]See note. 14.

[16]Daniel K. Roberts, "Freedom from Homosexuality: The Third Option," *Interaction : Newsletter of Association for Religious & Value Issues in Counseling* 13(1, Winter 1986), p.4 issued as a reprint by *Quest*. Atheism, literally "without god" or "without the need of god". Today it is defined, by American Atheists, as "the mental attitude which unreservedly accepts the supremacy of reason and aims at establishing a lifestyle and ethical outlook verifiable by experience and the scientific method, independent of all arbitrary assumptions of authority and creeds." Madalyn Murray O'Hair, Ph.D., one of the organization's most learned thinkers has argued numerous times that an individual's ability to transform the world culture by individual efforts is a commitment that is the very essence of life-assertion and is the ultimate glorification and praise of existence. Unfortunately many Americans, including Cook, believe or suggest that Ms. O'Hair is the founder of atheism in America. This shows a lack of historical knowledge and insight, for Emmanuel Julius (30 July 1889-31 July 1951) issued a series of books beginning with *Studies in Rationalism* in 1925. All he did was confirm ancient thought going back to Thales (640 BCE), Bias (608/583 BCE), and Anaximenes (548 BCE); see Madalyn [Murray] O'Hair, "Greek Roots of Atheistic Philosophy," *American Atheist* 29(1, January 1987), pp. 34-35, 44, quoting D.M. Bennett, following the text of American Atheist Radio series program No. 247, first broadcast on 1 June 1973.

[17]Roberts, *loc. cit.*

[18]*Ibid.*Genital love has historically been the foundation of all faiths, including Christianity in its pristine purity before it was corrupted by "Church Fathers" who were not only misogynistic and gynophobic but were so opposed to any form of sexuality that they forbade it altogether, basing their objections of Paul's injunction "that it is better to marry than to burn" but "far better" to be chaste in "the Lord." See Richard Payne Knight, *A Discourse on the Worship of Priapus, and Its Connection with the Mystic Theology of the Ancients ...to which is added an Essay on the Worship of the Generative Powers During the Middle Ages of Western Europe* ([London] Dilettanti Society, 1786; reissued Secaucus, NJ, 1974), and Reay Tannahill, *Sex in History* (New York, 1980). On the misuse of sex in Christian fundamentalism, see my *Unholy Rollers: Televangelism and the Selling of Jesus* (Arlington, 1985), and my *Evangelical Terrorism: Censorship, Fal-*

well, Robertson & the Seamy Side of Christian Fundamentalism (Irving, 1986). Male collaboration against the female sex began with the initial injunction that a woman was "created for man," even though the Genesis narrative states that "she" was created from the "rib" so that "she" would be the equal of man. Saul of Tarsus increased this gynophobia by arguing that women "must keep silent" (I Cor. 14:34-35), and that "wives, be subject to your husbands" (Col. 3:18)--husbands who were to be viewed as being the vicars (or substitutes) of and for "the Lord" (Eph. 5:22). Clement of Alexandria admitted his phobia, but attempted to sustain and support it by claiming that a "beard is then the badge of a man" and because of it "is active" and dominant. His student, Origen (185-254 CE) argued that "God does not stoop to look upon what is feminine" while Dionysius (190-264 CE) continued the Hebraic argument that "God will not heal her [of her] impurities" which are demonstrated by menstrual flow. Although Origen castrated himself to avoid sex, others took to standing in cold water, banning women from public rooms, and concentrating on "prayer lest they be tempted." These are discussed in my *Woman as Priest, Bishop & Laity* (Mesquite, 1984), pp. 61-102, with the documents given in English translation (Clement is to be found in *Pedagogus* 3.3; Origen in *Selecta in Exodus* 18:17 in Migne, *Patrologia...Graeca* 12:296f and Dionysius in Canonical Epistle 2, in *ibid.*). See my *Christian Fundamentalism, Sex, the Bible & Reality* (Athens, 1983) [in Greek and English]. An appreciation of the extent of Christian fundamentalist gynophobia and abuse of women is imperative since Cook alludes to homosexuals being like women and pyschologically impressed by women since "it is often expressed in a mother's close, binding relationship with a child (particularly if the father is emotionally distant or absent) and in the child's subtle manipulation of that relationship. The result, years later, is a diminished respect of the world of women."

"I well remember adolescent impressions...that women were not as intelligent as men.... That kind of distorted view limits emotional sharing with women and true sexual intimacy, because when we feel insecure in ourselves, we look for strength in our partner and feel put off by weakness." Therefore, male homosexuality is the result of a weak, "gossiping" and "giggling" mother!

[19] Roberts, *loc. cit.*

[20] Collins, *loc. cit.*; *Metanoia* [Seattle, WA], *loc. cit. Christianity Today* (21 September 1984), pp. 56-58.

[21]Cook has sent me numerous clippings and reprints. In each case his name or that of his organization has been highlighted with a yellow pigmentation.

[22]Not only does Cook condemn Boswell, but also Jesuit John McNeil (author of *The Church and the Homosexual*, New York, 1976, reissued, 1985), and Derrick Sherwin Bailey (author of *Homosexuality and Western Tradition*, London, 1955). He continues the same objections that have historically been leveled against gays (see my *City of Sodom & Homosexuality in Western Religious Thought to 600 CE*, Dallas, 1985, and my *Gomorrah & the Rise of Homophobia*, Las Colinas, 1985), that it is the result of indifferent parents, especially distant fathers and giggling mothers if the male becomes gay, or a frustrated mother and elusive father if the female's orientation is lesbian in nature. See "The H Connection."

[23]Beth Spring, "These Christians are Helping Gays Escape from Homosexual Lifestyles," *Christianity Today* (21 September 1984), p. 58. For a counter to this argument see James R. Smith, "Silent No More: Rev. John J. McNeill's Time to Speak Out," *The Advocate* (Issue 465, 3 February 1987), pp. 28-29, 64-65; and, in the same issue, Stuart Timmons, "Gays & Spirit; Part 2: Mainstream Turbulence: Stumbling Blocks in Traditional Religious Paths," pp. 29-33. See also, *Homosexuality and the Magisterium*, ed. John Gallagher (New York, 1985) for documents. Gay Jews have also been ignored, but equally have a rich and varied history; a recent article is by James M. Saslow, "Hear, O Israel: We are Jews, We are Gay," *The Advocate*, no. 465, pp. 38-41, 44-49, 108-111.

[24]"The H Solution," p. [16; back page].

[25]*HA News* (April, 1986), p. [1].

[26]*Ibid.*, p. 3.

[27]*Ibid.*.

[28]*Ibid.*.

[29]*Ibid.*.

[30]Published in Boise, Idaho, 1985, 48 pgs.

Chapter Two

Homosexuality: An Open Door?
Cook's Book

Colin Cook, the father of two boys,[1] argues that "the person in homosexuality [*sic*,] thinks about God, himself, and the world in a distorted way."[2] This "distortion" is generated, Cook argues, because the individual does not, will not, or cannot accept the Protestant Christian bible along the fundamentalist lines of Cook's readings and education received at fundamentalist Seventh Day Adventist Andrews University in Michigan.

To guide the homosexual "seeking recovery" from the "disease of homosexuality," Cook advises the neophyte to keep a journal "perhaps about 4 x 7" in size.[3] The journal is not to be a diary, but instead a transcript of "an honest coversation you have always wanted to have with a friend or family member."[4] The writing of the journal is to be helped with the purchase of a tape recording filled with Cook's interpretation of "the Christian message"–a taped recording of ten cassettes "offering a biblical, Christian solution to homosexuality."[5]

To lend an air of "authority" and "professionalism" to his statements against homosexuality, Cook calls upon an Elizabeth R. Moberly who has changed observable, clinical psychology into a circus of Christian vodooism.[6]

The initial message expounded by Cook is one encouraging self-doubt. He orders the "patient" to "think back" when the homosexual was a mere child and to appraise whether or not he/she had a comfortable and loving relationship with both parents. If there was no love in the primary familial unit, Cook argues, then the seeds of destruction towards becoming, allegedly, a homosexual were sewn. This view of the etiology of homosexuality was especially current and in vogue during the 1960s—when Colin was wrestling with his own homosexuality and homophobic training and education. Such a view was current with Lucy Freeman and Martin Theodores, who held that homosexuality is a "self-damaging" behavior that sadomasochistically developed in a personal quest for punishment,[7] because, as detailed earlier by Kurt Freund and V. Pinkava, the father was either intolerant, unconcerned, or rude, and the mother was sad because the child's gender was not the sex wanted of the newborn infant.[8] Neither "authority," however, discounts that homosexual behavior which is common among most species of animals—none of which has "parents" who have attitudes or sociosexual maladjustment like human mortals.[9] Homosexual animals do not have "retrojection complex" that professional psychologists and psychiatrists have attempted to label *homo sapiens* with since the 1950s[10] and before.[11]

Cook also argues that children who are given too much or not enough love become homosexuals men and women,[12] in harmony with random thought current in the 1950s.[13] This argument cites "crossdressing" by parents and permissive parenting which permitted a child to "play act" the role of the opposite gender.[14] What these thinkers on the value and impact of "role-playing/modeling" have ignored in their attempt to explain homosexuality as the result of "family backgrounds" is that not all masculine/dominative/aggressive homosexuals came out of authoritarian households any more than "feminine" homosexuals came from homes with a high degree of feminine identification.[15] Wainwright, and others, have rightly concluded that general sex-negativity ("erotophobia" or "homoerotophobia") is the result of culture in a phobic attempt to dictate and then control moral legislation and expression.[16] It is not a result of narcissistic impulses, or because male gays seek fellatio only because of their "inability" to perform autofellatio, or as an extension of autoeroticism in female homosexuals who desire "mutual masturbation."[17] At the same time, in opposition to Cook's argument that homosexuality is the result of a father's indifference,[18] studies show not only the contrary thesis,[19] but that such "indifference" can be assuaged by peer play relationships,[20] and that to claim any single generative source of homosexuality is presumptive and erroneous.[21] If there is neurosis in the character of the homosexual, it is because of both social pressure and familial/social/religious/personal confusion,/limitation/antagonization which either limit or deny self-actualization, personal esteem and the acceptance of primary and secondary drives.[22] Homosexuality is *not* an enactment of what the homosexual desires/assumes/presumes/desires to be,[23] but homosexuality, instead, is the antithesis of personal deprivation and the glorification, celebration and attunation of personal growth in some individuals in mass society.[24] Homosexuality is an inborn trait, characteristic, proclivity, orientation, interest, and lifestyle,[25] it is not "learned," "taught," or acquired as many argue.[26] Lesbians, at the same time, reject social stereotyping, familial conditioning, and, like gay men, desire only to be their self and developing, contributing, worthwhile people interacting with peers, subordinates and superiors in a meaningful way as demonstrated in dialogue, action, contribution and involvement in the plethora of social interaction and involvement.[27]

It is society that determines the demonstrative nuances and developments of causal concepts and presentational enactments of "masculinity" and femininity."[28] These stereotypes, so heatedly and belabored by ontological confessiology of primary Christian fundamentalism, actually worked toward the destruction of psychological equillibrium and self-actualization. Christian fundamentalism can hurt and/or destroy mental/emotional sanity.

Lesbianism gives some women a sense of equality not afforded by fundamental Christian churches and religious groups.[29] The stereotype that lesbians are the product of unaffectionate mothers[30] and lack femininity[31] was debunked, rebuffed and rejected years ago.[32]

The "problems" homosexual men and women render society is not etiological or assessatorial, but rather problems society gives or creates itself because of its primary homophobia teachings and beliefs which tend to coerce homosexual males and females into developing a community subculture in which gays ban together for mutual dialogue, interpersonal relationship, protection, and identification. The intensity of the homosexual subculture depends upon the society's adversion, rejection, blackmail, degradation and abuse of the homosexual especially through pseudoreligiosity, security prohibitions, and tautological denials or incarcerations in any penal or institutional system.[33] Except for the societally demanded sexual inversion and/or social seclusion of many homosexuals, gay men and lesbians are "almost an exact parallel between the psychological and physiological life and development of the normal [heterosexual] man [sic.] and that of the [homosexual] invert."[34] Homosexuals, as a group, like their heterosexual counterparts, are like heterosexuals in every way: their abilities, ethical and moral conduct, physical traits, need for stable love relationships, and sexual awakenings, sexual needs, and sexual expressions are undeniably identical.[35] Problems develop when "born-again" Christians exhort homosexuals, telling them that they have a psychiatric disorder and that their "[homosexual] illness" causes a great deal of misery[36] —a misery few homosexuals are aware of by themselves.[37]

It is individuals like Cook who accentuate the difference, who create a false sense of shame and self-condemnation in the homosexual that psychologically and morally should never be. This is done in the verbal ejaculations of pseudoreligious individuals who allege that they communicate directly to a supreme being who is intolerant of difference, narrow in perspective, and limiting in choice—a godling more apt to be the tribal totem of a small, isolated group protected by a wilderness never crossed than by any universal deity whose magnificence is expressed in the plethora of diversity.

This fundamental Christian godling is a token of the love missing, again according to Cook, from a same-sex parent.[38] Although he disclaims any oedipal or electra complex as being the source of generating homosexuality in an individual, his written thesis discounts his declamation and instead holds the archaic concept up for veneration as the idol saluted by mental experts in the 1950s and 1960s.[39] Cook argues that the normal human sexual feelings that are a natural part of the homosexual are "misinterpreted as erotic" rather than seen as "very legitimate and God-given" heterosexual feelings that have been supplanted by immediacy for physical contact rather than interpreted as a statement for a heterosexual quest and union.[40]

Ironically Colin Cook declares that "Homosexuality, in essence, has nothing to do with sex."[41] It is, Cook argues, a quest to find the self—again in tune with the arguments of the 1940s and 1950s when homosexuality was termed a "disease" or "mental illness" by primary homophobes.[42] The problem with these writings and interpretations, now commonly rejected by the profession, is that the clinical researchers, analysts and reviewers could not separate the worlds of psychology. The problem was not that homosexuals could not live in a heterosexual world, but rather that they could not live in an antisexual world since sexuality was codified, staid, ossified and truncated to a minimal form of expression.[43] Homosexual "promiscuity" and inversion is only legend.[44]

Colin Cook not only believes sexual desire "or [the] wish to masturbate" is an attempt to "find and complete the self,"[45] but infers that sexual expression is the instrument of sin when it is homosexual in nature.[46] He repeats the homophobic interpretation of Leviticus 20:13 by citation without any detailed explanation.[47] There is no indication that he has any knowledge of the ancient languages nor of the period that the passage is in reference to. He summarily and arbitrarily suggests that it is homosexuality, and "that the persistence in homosexual activity will result in exclusion from the kingdom of Heaven"—for which Cook cites 1 Corinthians 6:9. In both cases Cook is not only wrong, but his exegetics and hermneutics on the passages is nonexistent.[48]

Leviticus is a statement of statutes and judgments placed upon a primitive polytheistic people. The key word, in Hebrew transliteration *to'ebah*, is most aptly translated as "abomination" and is used in reference to incestuous relationships which included the using of sex in religious worship. It was not written, as fundamentalists alledge, by Moses, but by reforming priests over a long period of time, with some chapters in the book itself now dated during the Babylonian exile (587-539 BCE) to 400 BCE, when Babylonian religion encouraged and included homosexuality as a means of supplecating the Babylonian deities who were similar in nature to the Hebraic gods that ultimately were defined to be a monotheistic being. The passage that Cook likes to boast about, Leviticus 20:13, is in fact taken from the Zoroastrian *Zend-Avesta,* specifically from a book called *Vendidad* (the Persians book of ritual purity), chapter 8, sections 31-32:

> O Maker of the material world, thou Holy One! Who is the man who is a Daeva [Devil or Satan]?
> Ahura Mazda answered: The man that lies with mankind as man lies with

womankind, or as a woman lies with
womankind, is the man that is a Daeva;
this one is the man that is a worshipper
of the Daevas, that is a male paramour
of the Daevas, that is a she-Daeva; that
is the man that is in his inmost self a
Daeva, that is in his whole being a Daeva; this is the man that is a Daeva before
he dies, and becomes one of the unseen
Daevas after death: so is he, whether he
has lain with mankind as mankind, or as
womankind.

The words are similar to that of the Levitican code:
"You shall not lie with mankind as with womankind"
(18:22) and *"If a man also lies with mankind, as he
lies with a woman"* (20:13). And the Zoroastrian
law is *older* than the Levitical prohibition by at
least one hundred years if not more.[49] The Hebrews
adopted this Zoroastrian prohibition as a means of
establishing/stablizing monotheism and ridding the
existing cult worship of the tribal Yahweh from its
temple prostitution that was too close to the nature
of the "pagan" or country/rural faiths surrounding
it—faiths to which many Hebrews converted. Judaism
did not exist—only preexilic Hebraism that was still
in the phase of formalization and laboring to establish
a written law and code of conduct. To accomplish
this the role of women was subordinated and patri-
archalism introduced (not without dissent and attempts to reject it), and by doing so homosexuality
was frowned upon.[50] Ritual purity and "otherworld-
liness" came to the foreground in an effort to combat
idolatry and cosmopolitan consciousness, leading not
only to the innovation of homophobia but also to es-
calating xenophobia and numerous other phobiae
which were introduced to erase disbelief, idolatry and
heresy or unorthodoxy.[51]

Not only does Colin Cook not understand the
fine points of the bible he pretends to be an expert
on, but he misquotes, mistransliterates and in error
gives false interpretation and conceptualizations. This

is common and regular with the founder of Homosexuals Anonymous, and follows even in his writings. Not only does he claim Leviticus 20:13 to be a sin, but he couples his denunciation of "homosexuality" by citing 1 Corinthians 6:9 as a statement that his godling excludes gays from "the kingdom of Heaven."[52]

I Corinthians 6:9 does not condemn homosexuals to perdition, nor does it cast gays out of heaven. Transliterating the Greek characters into English characters, the two key words that Cook feels justifies his autocratic pronouncement are *malakoi* and *arsenokoitai*. The Revised Standard Version (1946) loosely translates them into a single expression: "homosexuals." The Revised Standard Version, 2d edition (1971) goes further and mistranslates the words to be "sexual perverts." And Today's English Version broadly entones "homosexual perverts," while *The New English Bible* goes the farthest and renders "who are guilty...of homosexual perversion" which is definitely not in the original Greek text. In actual Greek *malakoi* means "soft ones" who were "male prostitutes with their male clients"—the injunction is not against homosexuality but heterosexual men or homosexual men who sell sex for the sake of sex and not for love. The majority of these *malakoi*, in fact, were heterosexuals who found the sale of their body an easy way of raising currency.[53] *Arsenokoitai* is neither "perverts" (*The New English Bible*) nor "sexual perverts" (Revised Standard Version, 2d. edition). Instead the word means "immoral people," or people who offend society for any reason from failure to pay taxes to speaking out during worship services.[54] If sex is involved it is in the form of salable prostitution, especially in the form of the worship of any non-Judaeo-Christian god.[55] Some of this condemnation, in fact, applied to the practice both of non-circumcision as well as to autocircumcision where the penis was taken into the mouth and the foreskin was bitten off.[56]

Colin Cook next brings in what he sees as Saul of Tarsus' condemnation of homosexuality that he finds in the first chapter of Romans "that everybody in the world has the habit of suppressing the truth about Gods (even Christians.")[56] Before he addresses verses 26-28, he reflects that Saul's initial greeting is an affirmation of the Genesis narrative where the primeval gods (the "god" of Genesis 1:1 is plural in number in all the ancient languages; the Hebrew gives it as *Elohim* or "many gods") create "male and female." The line is Babylonian and Sumerian in origin and has nothing to do with genetic genderization but is purification of species—*Adamah* or Adam is "masters of", while *Eva* or Eve is both subordinate and earth—as discovered on a tablet at Sippar dating from the 6th century BCE. There are numerous other ancient records which also tell this story, and they do not acknowledge any god genderizing *homo sapiens* (or people).[57] The only thing that Genesis 1:27 tells the scholar is that the "creation" (actually the lifting up of or evolution of) "human beings" was accomplished so that mortals would "be in the divine image as rational and thinking beings." Cook makes a massive leap of ontological faith by claiming that this "creation" was heterosexual! That hypothesis is to be found no where in the original texts and was not even a part of primary patrology.[58]

Rather than elucidating upon his concept that "creation" was exclusively heterosexual, Cook abruptly cuts off his discourse on Genesis 1:27 and rifles in on Romans 1:28 claiming that the two are interrelated, which they are not. If Cook had been more careful and diligent in his reading, he would have noted that Romans 1:26-27 is a statement to the Christians telling them of the different things that had taken place in the past. The key word is "gave." The Greek is emphatic: it is past tense. It is a review of what occured. The recompense that the ancients received was a venereal disease, probably syphilis or gonorrhea.[59] The "lust in their hearts" which did "dishonor to their own bodies" was not homosexual activity but the worship of false gods.[60] This comment, woven into Romans 1:22-25, and is introduced as "idolators" (which precedes "catamites" and "pederasts" in I Corinthians 6:9). Worship in the Rome of Saul was image oriented. The *para' phúsin* (or "that which is against nature") is Stoic in origin and reflects the growing stoic concept that peace comes with rationality which avoids and denies temporal passions and pleasures (anger, love, sex, etc.). Saul would have mortals live "above" nature— outside of anger and wrath (Ephesians 2:3), and not live dependent upon physiological needs and/or desires (Galatians 5:16).

The few expressions in the bible of the Jews and Christians that reflect on intimacy—an intimacy which existed when John the Beloved Disciple was permitted to lay his head upon Jesus' chest, and the comfort Mary Magdalene felt when allowed "to minister" to Jesus is gender free (or dual-sexual). No where is intimacy limited on the basis of gender or gender exploration, expression or sexuality latent or overt. Colin Cook, on the other hand, repeats himself at various times in stating as if he were the Christ that "homosexual activity is a sin"[61]—even though Jesus never once made any mention of homosexuality—or heterosexuality— either to condemn one or the other, or to praise and/or encourage either or neither. The only objections to homosexuality in men and/or women is in the micromentality of the clergy who would misuse scriptures of any faith to support their own homophobia or self-debasement by denying their own natural proclivities which may include homosexuality and its various forms of interpersonal expression. This is their problem. It is not the problem of the self-actualizing, self-realizing, self-fulfilled and confident gay man or woman who celebrates the reality of joyful living comfortable in their sexual identity, knowing that homosexuality is a part of nature's sexual expression, rather it is the problem of such homophobes as Cook who relegate appreciation and acceptance of a natural phenomena—such as homosexuality—to the blood-stained altars of Christian insensitivity where fundamentalist high priests raise drawn daggers of demonic, dragonic damnation to a dwelling that only their personal consciousness could invent, tolerate, or live in. Their quotations of scripture never include Jesus' own dicta that even hypocrits can cite the bible to "prove" their own poverty of charity, love, understanding, knowledgeability, and compassion. They receive their own rewards in their crumpled calloused words.

Cook argues that "the force behind homosexuality" is "Wrath, Sin, Law, and Death." He cites Romans chapters 5, 6, 7, 8.[62] He is convinced that these "forces" are the instruments of "Satan." He takes random verses out of context, twists and distorts their meaning, and transmorgifies basic comments into sinister supplications that don't exist. He claims the general statement of Romans 1:18 is a direct reference to homosexuality, whereas in reality it is a statement against "ungodliness and unrighteousness of men, who hold the truth in unrighteousness." The actual passage refers to the power of God at creation and the "eternal power of the godhead." He attempts to justify his contention that the verse is in direct reference to homosexuality by citing verses 24, 25, 26—which we have already discussed as being in reference to false gods, which like most of the faiths of the age dealt with image veneration and worship. To a strict monotheist the worship of an inanimate object representing an animate (spirit) being was unfathomable and unthinkable and therefore, along with Stoic reasoning, unnatural.

The same god that Cook argues condemns homosexuals and homosexuality had the unique position of publicly dying "as a homosexual." Cook writes: "Jesus died as a homosexual," cites Isaias 53 verse 5, which makes no such claim, and then merrily skips around to other random verses—never coming back to his initial thesis that Romans 5, 6, 7, 8, condemn homosexuality—which they don't.

Every "sin" that Cook finds in his bible he equates as being a definite reference to homosexuality. It is as if the bible was strictly, solely, only, and totally on and against homosexuality—and that the Jesus message was not to be a homosexual—a message the man Jesus never made, nor a message ever recorded by any of Jesus' followers.

When he has difficulty in making a logical transition from one biblical passage taken out of context to another distortion of biblical information, Cook jumps into an area he has demonstrated remarkably little knowledge or ability: psychology. He is quick to claim that homosexuals are neurotics, and pontificates "Understand that your mind experiences some degree of neurosis—a common factor in homosexuality."[63] This thesis had limited popularity in the 1960s[64] but was discounted before then,[65] and afterwards.[66] Interestingly enough while Cook disclaims and laments this "neurosis," at the same time he advocates a new "Christian" neurosis in which he courages the homosexual to fight god in a "holy argument."[67] This, uniquely, is defended with a citation of Romans 3:25.[68] The actual context is a statement that "all" people (Jews and Gentiles) are "under sin (*There is none righteous, no, not one: there is none that understands, there is no one who seeks god...*" (Romans 3:10f.). The text concerns human kinds interest and activity in living a earthly life, which is filled with passion for money, possessions, as well as sex. Thus he suggests it is better to marry than live in unrequited passion: "to burn" (I Corinthians 7:9), to eat rather than starve, and to be the best person possible living within one's self, rather than attempting, falsely, to be what one is not and has no true interest in being.

The only point Cook made that has substance and provability is that "denying the existence of certain feelings in hopes they will go away ... will not lead to release from its power."[6][9] Substitution is not replacement or discontinuation. It is slavery, a mindset, that is the ultimate goal of Christian fundamentalists who want gay people to give up their homosexuality and in its place "develop" a heterosexual outlook and struggle to continue in a heterosexual framework. "Resist"ance to homosexual feelings is not a cure nor a reality, since rejection of one lifestyle is not acceptance of a different life style that is neither comfortable or desirable to the "resistor." Yet, Cook puts this argument into his Christian framework, and adds to his bible the following words that God "in effect" says: "I do not charge your sinful nature, your homosexuality, against you any more. It has been condemned and punished in Christ, My only Son."[70] Once more Cook has Christ being gay—a homosexual who Cook argues is not to be permitted to enter into "the kingdom of heaven" which most theologies argue is the "home of Christ" where he "awaits the saved."

Even though Cook argues that "God said" that homosexuality is a "sin," there is no foundation for such a claim in the bible. The passages that he draws out to support his house of cards make no claim that the "condemnation" is from God or Jesus—instead the passages he quotes are the writings of legalists, scribes, and preachers, all men who other men have labeled as "holy men." Yet these men lusted, sinned, wenched, and whored as did most people (both prophets and priests were prone to take concubines, and religious zealots found little hesitancy in stooping to rape the wives of their enemies), and their condemnation is a reflection of their society—not the will of any deity.

Giving up homosexuality, according to Cook, is the ultimate act of "obedience to the One whose love to you creates love within you."[71]   This relinquishment is, at the same time, tied to mental blackmail, for Cook argues, again out of context, that the homosexual will be damned for his or her "lustful" and hateful thoughts as if they were equivalent to murder and adultery—and then cites Matthew 5:22, 28.[72] In both citations support for Cook's thesis is nonexistent. Matthew 5:22 is a statement condemning of anger and uncharitable words *without a cause*: "But I say to you, that whosoever is angry with his brother *without a cause* shall be in danger of the judgement; and whosoever shall say to his brother, Raca, shall be in danger of the council, but whosoever shall say, 'You are a fool,' shall be in danger of [immortal anquishment, or] hell fire." Sex is not even remotely connected with this "sermon on the mount." The same is true for the twenty-eighth verse which is applicable only, and exclusively, to *hetero*sexuals: "But I say to you, that whosoever looks on a woman with lust has committed adultery with her already in his heart." Homosexuality is not discussed or implied. This is the case with the majority of Cook's citations of scripture—they have no relationship whatsoever to homosexuality or homosexuals.[72] In nearly every case the anguishment felt by Saul is over worldly concerns and involvements (cf. Romans 7:14-16). The evil Cook feels,[73] is that which he has determined—not that which is. The tragedy of the situation is that he has burdened innocent good gay men and women with his own self-loathing.[74]

Cook argues that homosexuality is a denial of basic genderation of mortals. Gay people know that there are two genders: male and female. This is in keeping with his citation of Genesis 1:27.[75] This verse, a part of the Creation Narrative, does not, however suggest sexual action or sexual identification. It is but a statement of gender reality. Very few homosexual males or lesbians have any doubt concerning their gender or the function of their genitals. Individuals who have the psychology of one gender and the unfortunate genitals of a different gender are not gay, but only transsexuals who deserve and merit a gender change, compassion and understanding. They cannot help the fact that they were born with the wrong body that does not match their psychology or temperment. Therefore, women living in a man's body, or men living in a woman's body are in truth what they know that they are and not what the externals present. Transsexualism is no more a sin or an "evil" than is being gay, being a Republican, being a patriot or being a Christian or atheist. Quality and goodness come from self-acceptance, self-actualization and self-reliance: virtues that Cook would deny to people who do not measure up to his homophobic standards.[76] Cook is correct, in a way, when he states that Genesis 1:26-27 details that "God created man in his own image" but in the context that "man" is a plural noun (meaning "masters of") as the introductory entonation declares: "Let us make man in our image, in our likeness, and let *them* rule..." The Genesis account does *not* say "God said, 'Let us make heterosexual males and females, in our image as a male and female [androgynous?] god, and let them rule..." [77] Sex is not a part of the creation narrative: thus god *could have* made Adam and Eve, *as well as* Adam and Steve, or Ada and Eve. The scrolls themselves do not acknowledge the generation of a singular first male and equally singular first female. Plurality of genders and individuals or attributes is instead to be found.[78]

The strict literalism of Cook on homosexuality does not stop with an attack on the homosexual and gay lifestyle. Parroting platitudes punctuating the nineteenth century, Colin also comes out boldly against masturbation as an other form of "homosexual mind-set."[79]

Cook justifies condemning masturbation on the ground that masturbation falls short of "the intimate sharing of the whole person with someone of the opposite sex in a lifelong relationship." He ignores the fact that couples, both heterosexual and homosexual, who have a lifelong relationship do engage in mutual masturbation and other masturbatory expressions. His avoidance of this reality is such that it permits him to condemn any form of sex other than penial intromission intercourse of penis and vagina—and then for "the purpose" of "procreation."[80] Surprisingly, Cook does not drag out the fundamentalist-favorite biblical passage considered to be proof that god condemns masturbation—the account of Onan (Genesis 38.8-10). In part, it may be, Cook overlooked or rejected incorporating this legend in his arguement against homosexuality since most people today see the account of Onan as being a record of *coitus interruptus*, which many churches view as "birth control," rather than acknowledging that the "sin" of Onan was not the sexual act but instead Onan's refusal to obey the levirate law of marriage (raising up an heir to his dead brother; see Deuteronomy 25: 5-10). The Genesis account (like the accounts in Leviticus 15:16-17 and 22:4) is a text concerned only with ritual purity and impurities— and not with moral "wrongdoing." This is also the case with the references Cook cites on the issue of "homosexuality".

At the same time, even more surprising, Cook does not address the legendary issue of the "Cities of the Plains"—Sodom & Gomorrah. The men in the cities were bad.[81] But the evil of the men of the Cities of the Plains were not bad because of homosexuality. They were unfeeling rapists, which is an act of dehumanizing one human being by another: an act which occurs in prisons, and is generally perpetrated by heterosexual males who use the act not only for sexual release but also as a way to establish or "prove" their superiority over others and thereby establish a "pecking order" or "caste system."[82] Even Ezekial attests to this fact (16:49), when he reminds the Hebrews "that this is the sin of Sodom and of her sisters: pride, fullness of bread, and abundance; her inability to put forth her hand to the needy and poor...." Sex is never mentioned.

The actual story of the "sin of Sodom" is quite simple. The Bedouin Lot had taken up temporary residence in the city of Sodom. One evening, while sitting in the town gate, two men [who the fundamentalists call "angels"] came to meet him. He invited them to his home. They accepted. He didn't bother to tell anyone in the city about his guests— even though Lot would have had to have known that foreigners were feared, and it was customary that all foreign denizen and visitors register with the town fathers to give surety of their peaceful intentions. The news of their arrival spread rapidly. Then, "the men of the city, even the men of Sodom, compassed the house, both young old, *all the people* [in this case meaning: men and women] from every quarter" came to Lot's house and demanded their right to see his guests ("to know" in this case has no sexual connotation, as it has in Genesis 3:6-7; the Semites understood the word only in context, never in the abstract. "To know" would have meant some form of a registration (visual, verbal, or physical) of the foreigners— and only if they were considered offensive, weak, or potential enemies would there have been a possibility of a rape of the men by some of the men in the city. Yet even if this had been the case it could never be considered a gay rape. It could be termed a homosexual rape only if "homosexual" is defined as "same sex" and not as "sexually oriented towards a member of the same sex." It is wrong to argue that the people of the city of Sodom were initially seeking sex, or to interpret "to know," in this case, as being sexual.)

The first actual sexual expression in the Sodom

story is Lot's offer of his two virgin daughters "which have not known man." Lot was quite willing to sacrifice his young daughters to the passion he believed he saw in the people of Sodom, far more so than he was willing to break the bond of hospitality—a social grace and practice of the bedouin people which he would not dishonor regardless of cost. Besides, at this time—which is in keeping with Cook's philosophy on women—women were of marginal value and thus their defilement and pain would mean as little to him or his peers as did the rape and subsequent murder of the concubine of "a certain Ephraimite" who was "traveling though the territory of Benjamine" (Judges 12:25ff). The love of things and concepts has historically been far more important than a genuine love of people,[85] and so it was in the days of Lot—a man who would sacrifice his own daughters so that he could maintain a conditioned concept.

The fact that the men of Sodom were damned for their inhospitality and not for their reputed homosexuality can be seen in the other passages that mention Sodom in the bible. Isaias 1:10-11 links the men of Sodom with "vain sacrifices." Jeremias 23:14 associates Sodom with adultery and lies. Gospel references are to inhospitality to strangers and foreigners. Even in the apocryphal books the sin of Sodom is not homosexuality, but pride (Ecclesiasticus 16:8), general wickedness (Wisdom of Solomon 10:6-8), or a combination of the two (Wisdom 19: 13-14).

Sex being the "sin" of the City of Sodom does not appear in "holy writings" until 200 BCE - 200 CE, when the pseudonymous Pseudepigrapha lists "fornication and uncleanness" (Jubilees 20:5) refering to all forms of sex outside of marriage and not just homosexuality, and the claim that the men of Sodom "changed the order of things" (Naphtali 3: 4-5)—not by being homosexual but because of the desire of the men of Sodom to have sex with angels!

It is on the foundation of these spurious documents and extracanonical works that various writers of the books and letters which were codified as being a part of the Christian canon took their theme and composed their messages. The scholar can trace the condemnation of II Peter 2:4-8 back to Jubilees and Naphtali, and Jude 6-7 is a part of the Jewish legend of "The Watchers" that were smoothed out in Genesis 6:1-4: giants who came to the earth to seduce mortal women and then forfeited their angelic positions with the "sons of God" (Genesis 6:2). So much of the New Testament is built on past records, legends, and fairytales in an attempt to control the minds of the small radical group of separated Jews who delighted in the name of Jesus. (Thus the "strange flesh" referred to in Jude 6-7, is a direct reference to the giants in Genesis 6:2, while the "child-corruption after the sodomitic fashion" in 2 Enoch 10:4 follows other early Hebrew tales.[86])

Cook has written his book. Unfortunately it is so far from the actual words of the bible he claims he is commenting on in proof and defense of his homophobia, that Cook has dissettled, unnecessarily, too many good people by throwing them into the chaos of fear created out of his own literal fundamentalism. And there is a price to Cook's slaughter of the innocence of gay men and women, for he reminds his readers of other works he has produced which they can obtain by writing him.[87] It's great show!

34

NOTES

Christopher and Brennan. On the inside cover of his book, *Homosexuality: An Open Door?* (Boise, ID, 1985) Cook observes that he has "completed" his "own struggle" with homosexuality, and within the pages of the book discusses "the problem of homosexuality" from both a psychological and religious perspective. As this chapter will detail, Cook uses arguments from the 1940s through the 1960s in supporting his primary homophobia—which he alludes to as being a part of his parental conditioning. His thesis is that an inadequate homelife or relationship with the parents generate "the disease of homosexuality." Interestingly, Cook selects only those arguments which defend his thesis. He fails to note that the same arguments he uses have frequent conditional clauses that hypothesize homosexuality to be congenital and/or hereditary and thus cannot be eliminated by psychological means (see: Magnus Hirschfeld, *Sex Anomalies: The Origins, Nature and Treatment of Sexual Disorders*, rev. ed., New York, 1948, 538 pp.), and that homosexual behavior is dependent upon hormonal levels in the individual established around time of birth (see: D. Gregory Mayne, "Homosexuality," *British Journal of Psychiatry* 114(Jan., 1968):125)—yet which cannot be "cured" by an administration of hormones (see: Abraham Myerson and Rudolph Neustadt, "Essential Male Homosexuality and Some Results of Treatment," *Journal of Nervous and Mental Diseases* 102(2, 1945):194-196. Cp. William H. Perloff, "The Role of Hormones in Homosexuality," *Journal of the Albert Einstein Medical Center* 11(3, 1963):165-178. What Cook fails to note is that "no one has the answers" concerning homosexuality; see: Isadore Rubin, "Homosexuality: Conflicting Theories," 1960, reprinted in *The Third Sex*, ed. Isadore Rubin (New York, 1961):13-22.

Cook, op. cit., p. [7].

Ibid., p. 9.

Ibid..

Ibid., p. 10; cp. McIntyre, *loc.cit.*

Elizabeth R. Moberly, *Homosexuality: A New Christian Ethic* (Geenwood, SC; offered by HA in *HA News*, p. 2).

Cook, *ibid.*, p. 11. Lucy Freeman and Martin Theodores, eds., *The Why Report* (New York: 1964), p. 602.

[8]Kurt Freund and V. Pinkava, "Homosexuality in Man and Its Association with Parental Relationships," *Review of Czechoslovak Medicine* 7(1, 1961):32-40. This finding was based on the statements of homosexuals interviewed in a controlled (closed) environment (they were hospitalized in the University of Prague Psychiatric Hospital), being openly judged as being "mentally ill." In spite of the preconceived, preconcluded concepts and presumed-before-analysis hypothesis, the researchers discovered that it was impossible to demonstrate any association between parental deprivation (including the absence of either parent or a hostile parent-child relationship) and homosexuality. Other cases were similarly encumbered: conclusions were assumed before actual investigation and analysis, and in each case the "patient" was categorized as "ill" and/or "in need of treatment" before the interviews and testings; see: Allen Clifford, "The Meaning of Homosexuality," *Medical World* 80(1, 1954):9-16 (and reprinted in *International Journal of Sexology* 7(4, 1954):207-212) which is a spin-off of his earlier "The Problems of Homosexuality," *International Journal of Sexology* 6(1, 1952):40-42, in which Clifford argues (as Cook will later) that homosexuality is the result of a broken home, an absent or antipathetic father, which materializes in the male homosexual's excessive affection for his mother. This became the foundation for Eva Bene's "On the Genesis of Male Homosexuality: An Attempt at Clarifying the Role of Parents," in *British Journal of Psychiatry* 111(487, 1965):803-813, which was written after a short questionnaire was administered to 85 male homosexuals (and 84 married men) who were members of homophile clubs and organizations (the married men were selected from a hospital staff). The role of the father was highlighted in Cornelius Beukenkamp, "Phantom Patricide," *Archives of General Psychiatry* 3(3, 1960):282-288. On the other hand, Irving Bieber, "Advising the Homosexual," *Medical Aspects of Human Sexuality* 2(3, 1968):34-39, has argued that male homosexuals are confirmed in their sexual activity because of the mother having an inappropriately intimate relationship with the son. In some ways Bieber's argument is a direct antithesis to W. Ronald Fairbairn, "A Note on the Origin of Male Homosexuality," *British Journal of Medical Psychology* 37(1, 1964):31-32, who argued that homosexuals value the penis as a breast substitute because the mother is seen as a "castrator" by her expressions of affection. Fairburn's arguments are part of the thinking of Harry Gershman, "The Evolution of Gender Identity," *American Journal of Psychoanalysis* 28(1, 1968):80-90. More than a decade earlier, Renee Liddicoat had written bravely and well that instability in the

the family of the homosexual was pronounced only in a few instances, the seduction by either parent (cf. Donald G. Langsley, Michael N. Schwartz, and Robert H. Fairbairn, "Father-Son Incest," *Comprehensive Psychiatry* 9(3, 1968): 218-226) was rare, and that homosexuals are as stable as society will allow homosexuals to be, in "Homosexuality: Results of a Survey as Related to Various Theories" unpublished Ph.D. dissertation, University of Witwatersrand, Johannesburg, South Africa, 1956, in direct opposition to H.W. Secor, "What Causes Homosexuality?" *Sexology* 16(4, 1949):226-232. It should be noted, however, that Secor's work does give covert reasons for some homosexuals accepting a non-positive attitude towards homosexuality and personal lifestyle: social intimidation, fear of intimacy because gender specification is given near canonical status, and loneliness which results because of social crassness and lack of civil charity.

[9]Karl M. Bowman and Bernice Engle, "The Problem of Homosexuality," *Journal of Social Hygiene* 39(1, 1953):2-16, argues that male homosexual relationships are more common in many cultures at all periods of time among both human beings and animals than are lesbian relationships. Bowman and Engle, however, argue that this natural phenomena can be arrested (or "cured") in human beings if the father is aggressive and assertive and "restrains ...[the boy's] instinctual drives" while the mother should offer "warm care" and affection, even though both authors acknowledges homosexuality to be both natural and normal. On homosexuality in animals see Wainwright Churchill, *Homosexual Behavior among Males: A Cross-Cultural and Cross-Species Investigation* (New York, 1967), and George Hunt and Molly Hunt, "Female-Female Pairing in Western Gulls (*Larus occidentalis*) in Southern California," *Science* 196(1977):81-83. The fact that homosexuality occurs in "every type of animal" has led R.H. Denniston, "Ambisexuality in Animals," in *Sexual Inversion: the Multiple Roots of Homosexuality*, ed. Judd Marmor (New York, 1965): 27-43, to write an internally contradictory paper, acknowledging the homosexuality in animals, but using mortal values to conclude that animals are socially conditioned to homosexuality. Claude E. Forkner, *et al.*, "Homosexuality," *New York Medicine* 10(11, 1954)'455-473 had concluded earlier that homosexuality is normal among all species, but, as Denniston would conclude later, it could be changed by oppressive sociological factors. Ancient scholars had long noted homosexuality in both the animal and mortal being worlds. For recent scholarship on this issue, see John Kirsch and James Rodman, "The Natural History of Homosexuality," *Yale Scientific Magazine*

51(3, 1977):7-13. The phobic concept of homosexuals being afraid of contact with members of the opposite sex has been discredited by most modern research; see: Kurt Freund, "The Female Child as Surrogate Object," *Archives of Sexual Behavior* 2(1972):119-133, and Kurt Freund, Ron Langevin, *et al.*, "The Phobic Theory of Male Homosexuality," *Archives of Internal Medicine* 134(1974):495-499.

[10]Daniel G. Brown, "Childhood Development and Sexual Deviations," *Sexology* 28(7, 1962):476-480 is among the articles most given to reiterating stereotypes: that children become homosexuals when there is a prolonged separation of the sexes, exciting and gratifying homosexual experiences during childhood are not caught and admonished, seduction by adult homosexuals, and threatening and painful experiences with the opposite sex. A year later Brown argued that male homosexuality is the result of a father who is usually either weak, passive and ineffective or is abusive, hostile, rejecting, and indifferent to his son (in his "Homosexuality and Family Dynamics," *Bulletin of the Menninger Clinic* 27(5, 1963):227-232), a theory initially presented by Gustav Bychowski, "The Ego and the Introjects," *Psychoanalytic Quarterly* 25(1, 1956):11-36, a highly theoretical application of Freudian psychoanalysis.
     W. Norwood East, "Homosexuality," *Medical Press* 217(Sept. 3, 1947):215-217, had earlier argued that homosexuality is the result of both genetic and environmental factors, a thesis rejected by Harold Eugene Edwards, "The Relationship Between Reported Life Experiences with Parents and Adult Male Homosexuality," unpublished Ph.D. dissertation, University of Tennessee, 1963.

[11]Marshall C. Greco, "Social Psychological Differentials in the Initiation and Retention of Chronic Homosexuality," *American Psychologist* 1(7, 1946):240. Otto Fenichel, *The Psychoanalytic Theory of Neurosis* (New York, 1945). J.D. Denford, "The Psychodynamics of Homosexuality," *New Zealand Medical Journal* 66(Nov., 1967):743-744. Louis A. Lurie and Carl H. Jonas, "Causes of Homosexuality," *Sexology* 11(12, 1945):743-746.

[12]Cook, *loc. cit.*. Cp. Harry Gersham, "Psychopathology of Compulsive Homosexuality," *American Journal of Psychoanalysis* 17(1, 1957):58-77, concludes that "compulsive homosexuality" is the result of an acquired conflict relating to the whole person generated by alienation by society and peers, compartmentalization, and externalize personal emptiness forcing the homosexual into massive self-resigna-

tion. Francis Pasche (in W.H. Gillespie, Francis Pasche, and George H. Wiedeman, "Symposium on Homosexuality," *International Journal of Psycho-Analysis* 45(2-3, 1964):203-216) argued at the 23rd International Psycho-Analytic Congress in Stockholm (July-August 1963), that male homosexuality can take four forms (repressed, fantasied, manifest, and sublimated) dependent upon parental response to emotional needs of children, while Wiedeman of New York rejected this and other "single cause" theories on the origination of homosexuality, arguing that sexual identity is determined in the first two or three years of life (*ibid.*). The role of the family is discussed in Kingsley Davis, "Sexual Behavior," in *Contemporary Social Problems*, ed. Robert K. Merton and Robert A. Nisbet (2d ed., New York, 1966):322-372, a thesis which has an unacknowledged debt to Lauretta Bender and Samuel Paster, "Homosexual Trends in Children," *American Journal of Orthopsychiatry* 11(1941):730-743. The idea that Cook has, and which has been expressed by several prominent psychologists of the 1960 era that homosexuals should marry as a means of "curing" their homosexuality, has been lucidly presented in Clifford Allen's contribution "When Homosexuals Marry," (1957), reprinted in *The Third Sex*, pp. 58-62 on why it won't work.

[13] Daniel G. Brown, "Inversion and Homosexuality," *American Journal of Orthopsychiatry* 28(2, 1958):424-429, no. 331. Medard Boss, *Meaning and Content of Sexual Perversions: A Daseinsanalytic Approach to the Psychopathology of the Phenomenon of Love*, trans. Liese Lewis Abell (2d ed., New York, 1949). Cp. Leon J. Saul and Aaron T. Beck, "Psychodynamics of Male Homosexuality," *International Journal of Psycho-Analysis* 42(1-2, 1961):43-48.

[14] Barry M. Dank, "A Social Psychological Theory of Homosexuality and Sex-Role Learning," unpublished Master's thesis, University of Wisconsin, 1966, is based on Orville Brim, "Family Structure and Sex-Role Learning by Children," in *Sociometry*, 1958. Cf. Albert Ellis, "The Sexual Psychology of Human Hermaphrodites," *Psychosomatic Medicine* 7(2, 1945):108-125, and Ralph J. Erickson, "Male Homosexuality and Society," *Bulletin of the National Association of Secondary-School Principals* 45(Nov., 1961):128-134. Cp. J.A. Hadfield, "Origins of Homosexuality," *British Medical Journal* (5486, 1966):678 argues that early childhood experiences help shape sexual identities, while John L. Hampson, "Deviant Sexual Behavior: Homosexuality, Transvestism," in *Human Reproduction and Sexual Behavior*, ed. Charles W. Lloyd (Philadelphia, 1964):498-510 takes the most zealous stand against

childhood play that is cross-genderized, since, Hampson argues at length, gender roles are determined by social learning during the earliest years of a child's life. This view is not totally accepted by Samuel B. Hadden, "The Psychotherapy of Homosexuality, 2. Group Psychotherapy in Homosexuality," *Psychiatric Opinion* 4(2, 1967):9-12, who writes that the psychology of a child is shaped by same-gender-peer interaction, and if a child is not permitted to play with his/her own peer group (age, social level, etc.), that child will, allegedly, develop a derogatory self-image. This thesis, like its predecessor, has been rejected by other researchers in the late 1970s.

[15]Classic studies which support this theory include, Harry W. Crane, "The Environmental Factor in Sexual Inversion," *Journal of the Elisha Mitchell Scientific Society* 61 (Aug., 1945):243-248, and Helen Mayer Hacker, "The New Burdens of Masculinity," *Marriage and Family Living* 19(3, 1957):227-233. The problem with this is in the interview processes which did not take into consideration the potential or possibility that the "homosexual" involved was acting out homosexuality in quest of attention, some form of reward, or self-punishment. Donal E. MacNamara, "Male Prostitution in an American City: A Pathological or Socio-Economic Phenomenon?" (paper read at the American Orthopsychiatric Association Meeting, 18 March 1965, in New York City, and mimeographed (8 pp.), notes that stereotyping human behavior can flaw analysis (none of those interviewed were alcoholic or addicts, only six of the thirty-seven were from broken homes, etc.). Sometimes, even in psychoanalysis, the researcher-counsellor has had to conclude that homosexuality is not only the actual psychology of the patient, but actually is better for the patient than schizophrenic heterosexuality; see: Eugene B. Brody, "From Schizophrenic to Homosexual: A Crisis in Role and Relating," *American Journal of Psychotherapy* 17(4, 1963):579-595.

[16]Wainwright Churchill, *loc. cit.* Eugene W. Green and L.G. Johnson, "Homosexuality," *Journal of Criminal Psychopathology* 5(3, 1944):467-480. One of the earliest studies on the normalty of homosexuality is W. Lindesay Neustatter, "The Homosexual Offender," *Justice of the Peace and Local Government Review* 123(30, 1959):480-481, which urged that the recommendations of the Wolfenden Committee Report (*Report of the Committee on Homosexual Offenses and Prostitution*, presented to Parliament by the Secretary of State for the Home Department and the Secretary of State for Scotland by Command of Her Majesty September 1957 ; re-

printed by Greenwood Press of Westport, CT in 1976; 155pp. and includes summaries of local findings and comparisons with other nations) to decriminalize homosexual acts. Isadore Rubin issued a similar call in his "Our Outmoded Sex Laws," 1960, reprinted in *The Third Sex*, ed. Isadore Rubin, *op. cit.*, pp. 102-106. Sweden had legalized homosexual acts years earlier, provided that the homosexual did not approach children or adolescents (see: Gosta Rylander, "Treatment of Mentally Abnormal Offenders in Sweden," *British Journal of Delinquency* 5(4, 1955):262-268, since homosexuality, in Sweden, is considered "abnormal" only when present in schizophrenia, imbecility, or severe anxiety neurosis.

[17]The argument that male homosexuals seek fellatio only because of their inability to perform autofellatio is the thesis of Frank S. Caprio, *Variations in Sexual Behavior: A Psychodynamic Study of Deviations in Various Expressions of Sexual Behavior* (New York, 1955) 344 pp. Gustav Bychowski has argued, "The Ego of Homosexuals," *International Journal of Psycho-Analysis* 26(3-4, 1945):114-127, that homosexuals are compelled by ego attempts to overcome pre- and post-natal narcissism. Individual acts, such as autofellatio, have occured also in the heterosexual world when heterosexual outlets have not been available (see: Leonard H. Gross, "Lesbians in Prison," *Sexology* 34(7, 1968):478-481; cp. Martin Hoffman, *The Gay World: Male Homosexuality and the Social Creation of Evil* (New York, 1968), 212 pp., and Th. G. Kempe, "The Homosexual in Society," *British Journal of Delinquency* 5(1, 1954):4-20. Evelyn Hooker, "Male Homosexuality," in *Taboo Topics*, ed. Norman L. Farberow (New York, 1963), pp. 44-55 acknowledges that among the greatest difficulties researchers realize in investigating homosexuality is the general reluctance of homosexual to be interviewed since many interviews are seen as working against the homosexual, entrapping the homosexual, or labeling the homosexual according to heterosexual stereotypes. The homosexual community provides not only social contacts for like-minded, like-oriented gays, but offers relatively strong and enduring friendships (see: Maurice Leznoff and William A. Westley, "The Homosexual Community," 1956, reprinted in *The Problem of Homosexuality in Modern Society*, ed. Hendrik M. Ruitenbeek (New York, 1963), pp. 162-174, and in *Sexual Deviance*, ed. John H. Gagnon and William Simon (New York, 1967), pp. 167-184.

[18]Cook, *op. cit.*, p. 11. Cp. Malvina W. Kremer and Alfred A. Rifkin, "The Early Development of Homosexuality: A Study of Adolescent Lesbians," paper read at the meeting of

Ameri

the American Psychiatric Association (Boston, MA, 13-17 May 1968), and printed in *American Journal of Psychiatry* 126(1, 1969):91-96. Cf. Max Hammer, "Homosexuality and the Reversed Oedipus Complex," *Corrective Psychiatry and Journal of Social Therapy* 14(1, 1968):45-47; and, Helen Mayler Hacker, "The Ishmael Complex," *American Journal of Psychotherapy* 6(3, 1952):494-512.

[19]M.S. Bird, "Some Emotional Problems Dealt with in the Special Clinic," *British Journal of Venereal Diseases* 41 (Sept., 1965):217-220. Parental relationships with the child/ adolescent only gives strength to variant amounts of self-identification/actualization, but does not create homosexuality; see Margery H. Krieger and Philip Worchel, "A Test of the Psychoanalytic Theory of Identification," *Journal of Individual Psychology* 16(1, 1960):56-63; cp. R.O.D. Benson, *In Defense of Homosexuality, Male and Female: A Rational Evaluation of Social Prejudice* (New York, 1965) 239 pp., and Marvin K. Opler, "Anthropological and Cross-Cultural Aspects of Homosexuality," in *Sexual Inversion: The Mutlple Roots of Homosexuality*, ed. Judd Marmor (New York, 1965), pp. 108-123.

[20]Samuel B. Hadden, "Etiological Factors in Male Homosexuality," in *Proceedings of the IV World Congress of Psychiatry*, Madrid (Sept. 5-11, 1966), pp. 3067-3069 (International Series no. 150; New York, 1967-1968), and his "Male Homosexuality," in *Pennsylvania Medicine* 70(Feb., 1967):78-80.

[21]Evelyn Hooker, "Homosexuality," in *International Encyclopedia of the Social Sciences* (New York, 1968), pp. 222-233.

[22]Charles R. Hulbeck, "Emotional Conflicts in Homosexuality," *American Journal of Psychoanalysis* 8(1, 1948):72-73. Carl H. Jonas, "An Objective Approach to the Personality and Environment in Homosexuality," *Psychiatric Quarterly* 18 (4, 1944):624-541. Alfred C. Kinsey, Philip Reichert, David O. Cauldwell and Eugene B. Mozes, "The Causes of Homosexuality: A Symposium," in *Sexology* 21(9, 1955):558-562; and, B. James, "Learning Theory and Homosexuality," *New Zealand Medical Journal* 66(Nov., 1967):748-751.

[23]The theory of ego-search for homosexuals was initially issued by Eugene A. Kaplan, "Homosexuality: A Search for Ego-Ideal," in *Archives of General Psychiatry* 16(3, 1967): 355-358, refinement of Nils Nielson, "The Riddle of Homo-

sexuality," *International Journal of Sexology* 6(1, 1952):51-53.

[24]Alfred C. Kinsey, Wardell Pomeroy, Clyde E. Martin and Paul H. Gebhard, "Concepts of Normality and Abnormality in Sexual Behavior," in *Psychosexual Development in Health and Disease*, ed. Paul H. Hoch and Joseph Zubin (New York, 1949), pp. 11-32

[25]John K. McCreary, "Psychopathia Homosexualis," *Canadian Journal of Psychology* 4(1950):63-74. Benjamin Glover, "Observations on Homosexuality Among University Students," *Journal of Nervous and Mental Diseases* 113(5, 1951):377-387. D.J. West, *Homosexuality* (Chicago, 1968). 304 pp. Alfred Kinsey, et al., *Sexual Behavior in the Human Male* (Philadelphia, 1948). Richard Green, "Homosexuality as Mental Illness," *International Journal of Psychiatry* 10 (March, 1972):77-98. Cp.Bayer, *op. cit.*, chap. 4.

[26]William H. Perloff, "Hormones and Homosexuality," in *Sexual Inversion: The Multiple Roots of Homosexuality*, ed. Judd Marmor (New York, 1965), pp. 44-59. John McLeish, "The Homosexual," *Medical World* 93(8, 1960):237-239; McLeish argues that "immature sexual relations" are not the sole property [sic.] of homosexuals, for the same immaturity can be found in heterosexual marraiges; immaturity is defined as the willingness to work at developing and maintaining an interpersonal/intrapersonal relationship.

[27]Simone de Beauvoir, "The Lesbian," 1952, reprinted in *Carol in a Thousand Cities*, ed. Ann Aldrich (Greenwich, CT 1960), pp. 181-205, and reprinted in *The Problem of Homosexuality in Modern America*, ws. Hendrik M. Ruitenbeek (New York, 1963), pp. 279-290. Lenore J. Weitzman, *Sex Role Socialization: A Focus on Women* (Palo Alto, CA, 1979), pp. 4-18. Jerrie Will, Patricia Self and Nancy Datan, unpublished paper presented at 82nd Annual Meeting of the American Psychological Association (1974). Carol Tarvis and Carole Offir, *The Longest War: Sex Differences in Perspective* (New York, 1977). Howard A. Moss, "Sex, Age and State as Determinants of Mother-Infant Interaction," *Merril-Palmer Quarterly* 13(1, 1967):19-26, 28, 30.

[28]Beauvoir, *loc. cit.* Tadeusz G. Grygier, "Psychometric Aspects of Homosexuality," *Journal of Mental Medicine* 103(432, 1957):514-525. Robert B. Dean and Harold Richardson, "On MMPI High-Point Codes of Homosexual Ver-

sus Hetrosexual Males," *Journal of Consulting Psychology* 30 (6, 1966):558-560. The influence of social consciousness and conditioning towards response reflexes (audio, verbal, stylistic and behavioral) is seen in Ralph F. Berdie, "A Femininity Adjective Check List," *Journal of Applied Psychology* 43(5, 1959):327-333. The entire concept of there being a "sexual spectrum" is the subject of A.L. Becker, "A Third Sex? Some Speculations on a Sexuality Spectrum," *Medical Proceedings* 13(4, 1967):67-74, which quite early acknowledges that some individuals can be biologically/physically male and yet psychologically female, yet assumes their sexual acts with other males to be "homosexual" inasmuch as the sexual apparatus is of the same gender, as well as some individuals who are biologically/physically female and psychologically male who prefer sex women are considered "lesbian"—and then acknowledges the reality of transsexualism, reviewing the psychodynamics of sexual identification, describing the extremes of hyperheterosexuality and how it can frequently mask the type of sexuality that society conditions as "homosexuality" on the sexuality spectrum. Unfortunately Becker's thesis falls short when he approaches the "treatment" stage of homosexuality.

[29]Edmund Bergler, "The Respective Importance of Reality and Phantasy in the Genesis of Female Homosexuality," *Journal of Criminal Psychopathology* 5(1, 1943):27-48, argues the standard that lesbianism is the result of experienced traumatic events in childhood. Bruno Bettelheim, "Growing Up Female," in *Psychoanalysis and Contemporary American Culture*, ed. Hendrik M. Ruitenbeek (New York, 1964), pp. 168-184 acknowledges the existence of conflict between individual interests and social conditioning based on gender, suggesting that some women will seek the company of their own sex so that they can be on a truly equal basis, freed of feelings of anxiety, inferiority, and disappointment. The destruction to normal psychology because of religious homophobia is in Michael J. Buckley, *Morality and the Homosexual: A Catholic Approach to a Moral Problem* (Westminster, MD, 1960) 214 pp., while Raymond de Becker, *The Other Face of Love*, trans. Margaret Crosland and Alan Daventry (London, 1967) examine the latent homosexual structure of Christianity and how homophobic homosexuals in the Church have attempted to subordinate this normal facet of life. Cp. my *Loving Women: A Study of Lesbianism to 500 CE* (Arlington, TX, 1986). The religious factor as encouraging homosexuality, especially among women, is the subject of Isaad Mohammed Atia and Mahoud Kamal Muftic, "Hypnosis in the Psychosomatic Investigation of Female Homosexuality," *British Journal of Med-*

ical Hypnotism 9(1, 1957):41-46; the authors note that the female in Moslem society is despised, mistreated, segregated in harems, and are considered objects because of a misogynistic body of holy writings (*Qu'ran*), leading them to suggest that there is a correlation between the rigidity and strictness of a religion (especially a fundamentalist ontology-theology) and the rate of homosexual activity among females.

[30]Harvey E. Kaye, et al., "Homosexuality in Women," *Archives of General Psychiatry* 17(Nov., 1967):626-634. Sylvan Keiser and Dora Schaffer, "Environmental Factors in Homosexuality in Adolescent Girls," *Psychoanalytic Review* 36(3, 1949):283-295. Cornelia B. Wilbur, "Clinical Aspects of Female Homosexuality," in *Sexual Inversion: The Multiple Roots of Homosexuality*, ed. Judd Marmor, pp. 268-281. Cf. Gilbert Van Tassel Hamilton, "Homosexuals and their Mothers," 1936, reprinted in *On the Causes of Homosexuality: Two Essays, the Second in Reply to the First* by Gilbert Van Tassel Hamilton and Gershon Legman (New York, 1950), pp. 5-15; cp. Alfred C. Kinsey, Wardell B. Pomeroy, Clyde E. Martin, and Paul H. Gebhard, *Sexual Behavior in the Human Female* (Philadelphia, 1953) 842 pp., and O. Martensen-Larsen "The Family Constellation and Homosexualism," *Acta Genetica et Statistica Medica* 7(1957):445-446.

[31]A part of the error that lesbians seek masculine roles and identification (while gay males are, allegedly, feminine) is because of the narrowness of the studies, most of which are based on select cases (prisons, mental institutions, etc.) and are not judged on a broad sampling, as is the case of Elizabeth M. Kates, "Sexual Problems in Women's Institutions," *Journal of Social Therapy* 1(4, 1955):187-191. Rose Giallombardo, "Social Roles in a Prison for Women," *Social Problems* 13(3, 1966):268-288, and her book, *Society of Women: A Study of Women's Prison* (New York, 1966) 244 pp., reject this claim, noting that most "prison lesbians" are heterosexual when not confined—a finding earlier reported by Seymour L. Halleck and Marvin Hersko, "Homosexual Behavior in a Correctional Institution for Adolescent Girls," *American Journal of Orthopsychiatry* 32(5, 1962):911-917. Cf. Edward Dengrove, "Homosexuality in Women," 1957, reprinted in *The Third Sex* ed. Isadore Rubin, pp. 23-27.

[32]Malvina W. Kremer and Alfred H. Rifkin, "The Early Development of Homosexuality: A Study of Adolescent Lesbians," (paper read at the meeting of the American Psychiatric Association, Boston, MA, 13-17 May 1968) printed in *Amer-*

ican Journal of Psychiatry 126(1, 1969):91-96, where the conclusion reached is that homosexuality may be a final common behavioral pathway rather than a single entity with but one etiology..

[33]Eugene B. Mozes, "The Lesbian," *Sexology* 18(5, 1951):294-299, thesis that lesbianism is a neurosis representing an arrest in sexual development (while acknowledging that there is no hormonal difference or difference in physical makeup, including secondary sex characteristics, between homosexuals and heterosexuals), has been rejected by David A. Ward and Gene G. Kassebaum, "Lesbian Liaisons," *Trans-Action* 1 (2, 1964):28-32, and Harvey Bluestone, Edward P. O'Malley and Sydney Connell, "Homosexuals in Prison," *Corrective Psychiatry and Journal of Social Therapy* 12(1, 1966):13-24; cp. William G. Miller and Thomas E. Hannum, "Characteristics of Homosexually Involved Incarcerated Females," *Journal of Consulting Psychology* 27(3, 1963):277. Cf. Marise Querlin, *Women without Men*, trans. Malcom McGraw (New York, 1965) 174 pp.

[34]Anomaly. *The Invert and His Social Adjustment: To Which is Added a Sequel by the Same Author* (2d rev. ed., Baltimore, MD, 1948) 290 pp..

[35]Charles Berg, "The Problem of Homosexuality," *American Journal of Psychotherapy* 10(4, 1956):696-708; 11 (1, 1957):65-79. Norman George Bills, "The Personality Structure of Alcoholics, Homosexuals, and Paranoids as Revealed by Their Responses to the Thematic Apperception Test," unpublished Ph.D. dissertation, Western Reserve University, 1953 228 pp.. Cf. Thomas R. Byrne, Jr. and Francis M. Mulligan, ' "Psychopathic Personality" and 'Sexual Deviation': Medical Terms or Legal Catch-Alls—Analysis of the Status of the Homosexual Alien," *Temple Law Quarterly* 40(4, 1967):328-347. Candidus, *The Nature of Man: The Problem of Homosexuality* (Cambridge, 1954) 7 pp. Kenneth Soddy, "Homosexuality," *Lancet* 267 (6837, 1954):541-546.

[36]Cook, *op. cit.*, p. 12. On the brutality of the Christian churches towards homosexuality and homosexuals, see: Robert Watson Wood, *Christ and the Homosexual: Some Observations* (New York, 1960) 221 pp.. Daniel Day Williams, "Three Studies of Homosexuality in Relation to the Christian Faith," *Social Action* 34(4, 1967):30-37, and H. Kimball Jones, *Toward a Christian Understanding of the Homosexual* (New York, 1966) 160 pp., cp. Ken Jackson, "HA Tries to

Help Gays Go Straight," *Tulsa World* (5 November 1985), p. A1, A4. Homosexuals Anonymous are coupling the AIDS tragedy, which is striking both heterosexual and homosexual men and heterosexual women (there are no reported cases of lesbians contracting AIDS in the United States or elsewhere), as being part of a divine plan that is affecting homosexual life-styles. For a more "traditional" Christian perspective, see the Episcopalian *Exodus Standard* (Seattle), which was organized "for Biblical Sexuality"—which, by its very standard and definition means that these Episcopalians encourage rape, incest and debauchery as practiced by Old Testament prophets while condemning homosexuality. See my comments below.

[37]Colin Cook, *God's Grace to the Homosexual* (Reading, PA: pamphlet); his *Homosexuality and the People of God* (Reading, PA: pamphlet; and, Meg True, *Homosexuality in the Family* (Reading, PA: reprint of two articles first appearing in *Review*. For an emotion-arousing diatribe on homosexuality and the threats of Colin's godling, see his *Which Door To Heaven?* (Reading, PA: pamphlet).

[38]Cook, *Homosexuality: An Open Door?*, p. 12. Cp. Robert Veit Sherwin in "Sex Society Forum on Homosexuality," *Sexology* 26(3, 1959):169. Cf. John J. McNeill, S.J., *The Church and the Homosexual* (New York, 1976, reissued 1985 without imprimatur).

[39]Rene Guyon, Wilfrid D. Hambly, Edwin W. Hirsch, Olivier Loras and Joseph G. Wilson, "The Causes of Homosexuality: A Symposium" *Sexology* 21(11, 1955):722-727. Magnus Hirschfeld, *Sexual Anomalies: The Origins, Nature, and Treatment of Sexual Disorders* (Rev. ed., New York, 1948) 538 pp. These theses have been questioned in Chuck Taylor, "The Successful Homosexual," *One* 7(5, 1959):5-9. Judy Chang and Jack Block, "A Study of Identification in Male Homosexuals," *Journal of Consulting Psychology* 24(4, 1960):307-310 hallmarked the 1960s, which has male homosexuals identifying with their mothers; however, Daniel G. Brown and David B. Lynn, "Human Sexual Development: An Outline of Components and Concepts," *Journal of Marriage and the Family* 28(2, 1966):155-162 shows that many homosexuals are not "inverted" in their sex or gender roles, nor identify with their mothers to the exclusion of fathers.

[40]Cook, *loc. cit.*

[41]*Ibid.,*

[42] Leslie W. Barnette, "Study of an Adult Male Homosexual and Terman-Miles M-F Scores," *American Journal of Orthopsychiatry* 12(April, 1942):346-352, has the most charitable view, with the author suggesting that his patient is well-behaved and does not generate problems for society since he is intellectually, socially, and artistically valuable. This charity is lacking in Lauretta Bender and Alvin E. Grugett, Jr., "A Follow-Up Report on Children Who Had Atypical Sexual Experience," *American Journal of Orthopsychiatry* 22(Oct., 1952):825-837, or that of Nathan J. Blackman, "The Culpability of the Homosexual," *Missouri Medicine* 50(1, 1953): 27-29. On the absurdity of classifying homosexuals according to the acts performed at any given time, see: Marvin H. Lipkowitz, "Homosexuality as a Defense against Feminine Strivings: A Case Report," *Journal of Nervous and Mental Disease* 138(Apr., 1964):394-398.

Among the most absurd arguments to come out of the 1950s is that by Louis S. London, *Abnormal Sexual Behavior* (New York, 1957) 427 pp., where homosexuality is adjudged to be a conflict of "acquired instinctive cravings" and religious training leading to general impotence. What London failed to see is the overwhelming damage done to his patient by his strict literalistic religious training and teaching, enchaining his psyche to biblical distortions and horatory homophobia.

[43] Donald Webster Cory, *The Homosexual in America: A Subjective Approach* (New York, 1951) 326 pp. argues that homosexuals should enter therapy for self-acceptance and in order to become better adjusted to society, since homosexuals live not in a heterosexual world, but one that is antisexual due to heterosexual homophobia. Cf. "DOB Questionnaire Reveals Some Comparisons Between Male and Female Homosexuals," *Ladder* 4(12, 1960):4-25. On the influence of heterosexual culture on homosexuals, see: Albert Ellis, "The Influence of Heterosexual Culture on the Attitudes of Homosexuals," *International Journal of Sexology* 5(2, 1951):77-79.

[44] Robert B. Dean, "Some Considerations on Promiscuity in Male Homosexuals," Mimeographed (Apr., 1967), a counter to M.S. Bird, "Some Emotional Problems Dealt with in the Special Clinic," *British Journal of Venereal Diseases* 41 (Sept., 1965):217-220. Cf. Liddicoat, *loc. cit.*, which notes that homosexual "promiscuity" is an invention of heterosexual homophobes; see its summary in *British Medical Journal* (5053, 1957):1110-1111.

[45] Cook, *op. cit.*, pp. 39-40, yet Cook advises the indi-

vidual "suffering" from homosexuality to "place yourself, submissively, before Psalm 139:13-17. "You created my inmost being; you knit me together in my mother's womb, I praise you because I am fearfully and wonderfully made." Verse 13, 14. *Then take off your clothes, stand before the mirror....*" (my emphasis). A most interesting suggestion on how to stop masturbation!

Homosexual guilt over masturbation was part of the doctoral dissertation of Richard Wallace Thomas, "An Investigation of the Psychoanalytic Theory of Homosexuality," Ph.D University of Kentucky, 1951, 167 pp. Cp. R.E.L. Masters, *Forbidden Sexual Behavior and Morality: An Objective Reexamination of Perverse Sex Practices in Different Cultures* (New York, 1962), 431 pp., which urges that sexual behavior should be defined according to what is dangerous and harmful to individuals and society and not just what is forbidden because it seemed undesirable to ancient Hebrew and Christian lawmakers. Robert J. Bledsoe, *Male Sexual Deviations and Bizarre Practices* (Los Angeles, CA, 1964) argues that practices like masturbation have always been with humankind (heterosexual as well as homosexual) and that no one can be termed 100 percent "normal."

[46]Cook, *op. cit.*, p. 13. This argument was presented by Patrick Devlin, "The Enforcement of Morals," (London, 1959; pamphlet) 25 pp., who argues that laws concerning sex must be based on Christian morals and Christians must enforce these laws otherwise Christian teachings against masturbation, homosexuality, and other "perversions" will fail. The barbarity of Judaeo-Christian "laws" on masturbation, homosexuality and other forms of "non-conventional sexuality" are discussed in Norman St. John-Stevas, *Life, Death and the Law: Law and Christian Morals in England and the United States* (Bloomington, IN, 1951) 375 pp.; for a rejoinder, see: John Wolfenden, "Evolution of British Attitudes toward Homosexuality," *American Journal of Psychiatry* 125(6, 1968):792-797.

[47]Cook, *loc. cit.*

[48]*Ibid.* Saul's objection to "the flesh," like many of his other caveats, is the result of his Stoic education which had traces of Indian ontology as it influenced Zoroastrian theology (see: G. Rattray Taylor, *Sex in History* (New York, 1973), p. 243. The term *pornoi* (πορνοι) in this case means "male prostitute" which, as understood in early Christian literature, was any person who indulged in any sexual relation considered irregular (not husband-wife penial intromission for procreation).

In most cases this act was an incestuous heterosexual relationship (as discussed in I Corinthians 5).

[49] *Zend-Avesta, Vendidad* 8.31-32, trans. James Darmesteter in Sacred Books of the East, Vol. IV: *The Zend-Avesta—Part I: The Vendidad* (1880; reprint, Delhi, 1965), Farg. VIII:31-32, pp. 101-102.

[50] Leviticus 18:19, 20. Cf. my *Woman in ancient Israel under the Torah and the Talmud* (Mesquite, 1978, 1982).

[51] Edward Westermarck, *The Origin and Development of the Moral Ideas* (1906; 2nd ed., London, 1917), vol. 1, p. 488.

[52] Cook, *loc. cit.*

[53] The reading of the verse in question resembles an old Roman game where "virtues" were placed on one side of a gaming board to be countered on the other side by the "vices" that were popular at the time. Eight of the ten "vices" that Saul condemns are on the counters of this particular game. Cf. Tom Horner, *Jonathan Loved David: Homosexuality in Biblical Times* (Philadelphia, 1978), p. 93. The word μαλακοι (or *malakoi*) is plural in number, and as defined by "Matthew" (11:8) and "Luke" (7:25) were passive holy men who accepted male intercourse as a means of pleasing their god—not necessarily because of their own preference or proclivity; these *malakoi* were the same as the *kedeshim* or "holy men" of the Old Testament who passively accepted anal intercourse to please their gods. The αρσενοκοιται (or *arsenokoites*) were again "holy men" but who took the active sex role to please the god(s). In both cases this is not to be read as exclusively homosexual holy men, as Horner states, but rather as heterosexual "holy men" who engaged in the pagan (country-like) worship of a deity as demonstrated in sexual (anal) intercourse tantamount to the expression of yin and yang. This form of male sexuality was prostitution—not homosexuality since the anal intercourse was engaged in for the pleasure of the deities and not the participants. To argue otherwise is only to show the western Christian to be prejudice without foundation or academic knowledge. See Hans Lietzmann, *Handbuch zum Neuen Testament* 1906; 4th ed. Tuebingen, 1949), vol. 9, p. 27; Derrick Sherwin Bailey, *Homosexuality and the Western Christian Tradition* (Hamden, CT, 1975), p. 38. In the non-theological world the words connoted other forms of pacifism (not necessarily sexual or political), but often as derogational.

⁵⁴η ουχ οιδατε οτι αδικοι Θεου βασιλειαν ου κληρονομησουσι μη πλανασθε• ουτε πορνοι ουτε ειδωλολατραι ουτε
μοιχοι ουτε μαλακοι ουτε αρσενοκοιται ουτε κλεπται ουτε
πλεονεκται ου μεθυσοι ου λοιδοροι ουχ αρπαγες βασιλειαν
Θεου κληρονομησουσι, the fact that there were male prostitutes who engaged in sex with men for money (and sold sex
to women for personal income) is the conclusion of this argument: ουκ οιδατε οτι τα σωματα υμων μελη Χριστου εστιν
αρας ουν τα μελη του Χριστου ποιησω πορνης μελη μη γενοιτο
η ουκ οιδατε οτι ο κολλωμεενος τη πορνη εν σωμα εστιν
Εσονται γαρ φησιν οι δυο εις σιαρκα μιαν. Note that the word
"harlot" is in the feminine, and thus is applicable to both
genders (since heterosexual male prostitutes frequently dressed
as women and played feminine roles to please their male
clients who came to them as a substitute when their women
were either pregnant, in child labor, gone, dead, or just want-
ing the "excitement" of a man while pretending the male
prostitute was a woman. Therefore the key to the condemnation is the words "as if"—since such conditions were seen as
rejection of actuality—not of sexual preference, a common
aspect of his ecclesiological-Christian society (in tune with the
social consciousness of his day; which condemned women to
silence (I Corinthians 14:34-35), but also sanctioned slavery
and encouraged slaves to be docile (Colossians 3:22: οι δουλοι
υπακουετε κατα παντα τοις κατα σαρκα κυριοις μη εν οφθαλ-
μοδουλειαις ως ανθρωπαρεσκοι αλλ εν απλοτητι καρδιας
φοβουμενοι του Κυριον...) Thus it is far better to read the verses
in question as "male prostitutes with clients" who engaged in
any sexual activity within a given social group which the re-
mainder of society considers societally unacceptable behavior
(or "abnormal": against the norm); see Clellan S. Ford and
Frank A. Beach, *Patterns of sexual Behavior* (1951, reprint
New York, 1972), p. 282, cf. pp. 125-143, when referencing
William Barclay, *The Letters to the Corinthians* (1954; 3d ed.,
Baltimore, MD, 1975), pp. 51-52.

⁵⁵Saul issued his concept of "false gods" and the sexual worship of these demideities in Romans 1:26-27: Δια
τουτο παρεδωκεν αυτους ο Θεος εις παθη ατιμιας αι τε γαρ
θηλειαι αυτων μετηλλαξαν την φυσικην χρησιν εις υην παρα
φυσιν ομοιως τε και οι αρρενες αφεντες την φυσικην χρησιν
της θηλειας εξεκαυθησαν εν τη ορεξει αυτων εις αλληλους
αρσενες εν αρσεσι την ασχημοσυνην κατεργαζομενοι και την
αντιμισθιαν ην εδει της πλανης αυτων εν εαυτοις
αποαμβανοντες. Notice the word "idolaters" precedes this
condemnation, as it does in I Corinthians 6:9. See Robert W.
Wood, "Homosexual Behavior in the Bible," *ONE Institute*

Quarterly 5(1, 1962):10-19. Cp. Joseph C. Weber, "Does the Bible Condemn Homosexual Acts?" in *engage/social action* 3(5, 1975)'34. McNeill, *op. cit.*, p. 42, argues that "The pervert is not a genuine homosexual; rather he is a heterosexual who engages in homosexual practices, or a homosexual who engages in heterosexual practices." Thus, being a "sodomite" is either gender pretending the individual to possess sexual proclivities and interests toward a gender it is sexually uncomfortable. Therefore, homosexuals who pretend to be heterosexuals and engage in heterosexual sexuality are perverts and not admissable to heaven.

[56]Circumcision is not natural, but rather a socially conditioned practice. Involuntary circumcision can leave a psychological disability on the victim; see: Melitta Schmideberg, "A Note on Homosexuality and Circumcision," *Psychoanalytic Review* 35(2, 1948):183-184, and Harry W. Crane, "The Environmental Factor in Sexual Inversion," *Journal of the Elisha Mitchell Scientific Society* 61(Aug., 1945):243-248. This may help explain Saul's verbal conflict with Simon bar Jonas (Peter) over the issue of circumcision in the fledgling church.

[57]Robert Graves and Raphael Patai, *Hebrew Myths: the Book of Genesis* (New York, 1963), pp. 1-34, 60-64.

[58]Cook, *op. cit.*, p. 14.

[59]R.R. Willcox, "Venereal Diseases in the Bible," *British Journal of Venereal Diseases* 15(1949):28-33, offers commentary and bibliography, while a brief (12 pages) survey is offered by Tom Horner, *Sex in the Bible* (Rutland, VT, 1974), especially pp. 104-108, discusses venereal diseases.

[60]Lust (or "covetousness") and idolatry (*eidololatrai* or εἰδωλοοατραι) is a statement of worshipping idols or any deity by veneration of images or immediacy of contact—a common aspect of theology in the Roman world of Saul and the early Christians. When Saul uses it in I Corinthians 6:9-10, it is done so in the same manner as his references in chapter 5: in both cases it is a condemnation of incestuous and idolatorous heterosexual relations. The majority of the men who went to the "sacred prostitutes" were married male men.

[61]Cook, *op. cit.*, p. 15.

[62]*Ibid.*, p. 17.

52

63*Ibid.*, p. 19.

64Coinage of such terminology became common after
the release of Rene Guyon, Wilfrid D. Hambly, Edwin Hirsch,
Oliver Loras, and Joseph G. Wilson's "The Causes of Homosexuality: A Symposium," *Sexology* 21(11, 1955):722-727. with
Edwin W. Loras rejecting the theory that homosexual tenden-
cies are inherited in his effort to substantiate the "neurotic
origins" thesis, which also found expression in W. Lindesay
Neustatter, "Homosexuality: The Medical Aspects," in *They
Stand Apart: A Critical Survey of the Problems of Homosexuality*, ed. John Tudor Rees and Harley V. Usill (London, 1955)
pp. 67-139. Among the most homophobic and unreasoning
papers published on the theory that homosexuality is "a sub-
division of neurosis," see Edmund Bergler, "What Every
Physician Should Know about Homosexuality," *International
Record of Medicine* 171(11, 1958):685-690, that was followed by P.J. O'Connor, "Aetiological Factors in Homosexuality
as Seen in Royal Air Force Psychiatric Practice," *British
Journal of Psychiatry* 110(466, 1964):381-391, and the out-
landish claims of Benjamin Kaplan, "The Structure of Neu-
roses: With Special Differentials Between Neurosis, Psychosis,
Homosexuality, Alcoholism, Psychopathy, and Criminality,"
Archives of Criminal Psychodynamics 4(4, 1961):599-646,
where the bottom line is the claim that homosexuality is
"definitely curable."

65Abraham Myerson and Rudolph Neustadt, "Bisexu-
ality and Male Homosexuality: Their Biological and Medical
Aspects," *Clinics* 1(4, 1942):932-957, argue that homosexuality can not be considered a disease (although it may form a
background for neurotic or psychotic symptoms), while Martin Roth and J.R.B. Ball, "Psychiatric Aspects of Intersexuality," in *Intersexuality in Vertebrates Including Man*, ed. C.N.
Armstrong and A.J. Marshall (London, 1964), pp. 395-443,
argue that while neurotics are found among homosexuals, so
too are normal personalities to be found among homosexuals.
That neurosis is equally found in heterosexuals and homosexuals is the thesis of E. Winterstein-Lambert, "Observations on
Homosexuals," *Bulletin de la Faculté de Médecine de Istanbul*
12(13, 1949):216-220.

66Daniel Offer and Melvin Sabshin, *Normality: Theoretical and Clinical Concepts of Mental Health* (New York,
1974), p. 90. Cf. Bayer, *loc. cit.*.

67Cook, *loc. cit.*.

[68]*Ibid.* The line, ον προεθετο ο Θεος ιλαστηριον δια της πιστεως εν τω αυτου αιματι εις ενδειξιν της δικαιοσυνης αυτου δια την παρεσιν των προγεγονοτων αμερτηματων εν τη ... is at best ambiguous.

[69]Cook, *ibid.*, p. 20.

[70]*Ibid.*, p. 21. Denial of sexuality, especially homosexuality, is and has been common in all homophobic cultures (see: G. Morris Carstairs, "Hinjra and Jiryan: Two Derivatives of Hindu Attitudes to Sexuality," *British Journal of Medical Psychology* 29(2, 1956):128-138, the "problem" of homosexuality lies with the society and not the individual homosexual (see: Churchill, *loc. cit.*., and G. Morris Carstairs and Tadeusz G. Grygier, "Anthropological, Psychometric, and Psychotherapeutic Aspects of Homosexuality," *Bulletin of the British Psychological Society* 32(1957):46-47.

[71]Cook, *ibid.*, p. 23. The errors in Christianity's attempt to "cure" homosexuality is the thesis of Robert L. Katz "Church History, Attitudes, and Laws," (unedited working paper prepared for the National Institute of Mental Health Task Force on Homosexuality) (Cincinnati, 1967; mimeographed) 15 pp. Societal interpretation of the merit or "sinfulness" of homosexuality has surfaced in John I. Kitsuse, "Societal Reaction to Deviant Behavior: Problems of Theory and Method," *Social Problems* 9(3, 1962):247-256, and Anthony Ludovici, "Homosexuality, the Law and Public Sentiment" *International Journal of Sexology* 5(3, 1951-52): 143-150, with a commentary by Clifford Adams. Ronald M. Mazur, *Commonsense Sex* (Boston, 1968) 109 pp. details how the persecution of homosexuals is reinforced by religious prejudices and the dominant heterosexual's image of manhood and "maleness." On society's role in surpressing the homosexual, see Elizabeth A. Rooney and Don C. Gibbons, "Social Reaction to 'Crimes Without Victims'." *Social Problems* 13(4, 1966):400-410.

[72]Cook, *loc. cit.* For an opposing view, see my *Gomorrah & the Rise of Homophobia* (Las Colinas, TX, 1985).

[73]Cook, *ibid.*, p. 30.

[74]*Ibid.*, pp. 16, 46. A classic case, similar in nature (although not exact in detail) is the story of El by Evelyn Hooker, "The Case of El: A Biography," *Journal of Projective Tech-*

niques and Personality Assessment 25(3, 1961):252-267. The fear and denial of homosexuality can lead individuals into neurotic situations and psychotraumatic problems: see: "Homosexuality," *GP* [*General Practioner*] 16(4, 1957):132.

[75]Cook, *op. cit.*, p. 35. The key thought in this passage concerns the image of the body which is thought of as special or "sacred" and thus a deliberate act of defilement of the body carries with it a vengeance upon the attacker (not the individual attacked) with total disregard for the being used or abused. The passage has nothing to do with homosexuality in its existing context. The issue is more towards rape and murder where the victim is not considered and the mere commissioning of the act is damned.

[76]Cook, *loc. cit.* Transsexualism is the engineered surgical process of changing one sexual apparatus for the sexual apparatus of the opposite gender. This is done so that the genitals of the individual will match with the psychology and attitude of the individual. See Leslie Martin Lothstein, *Female-to-Male Transsexualism: Historical, Clinical, and Theoretical Issues* (Boston, 1983) 336 pp. H. Baker and R. Stoller, "Can a biological force contribute to gender identity?" *American Journal of Psychiatry* (124, 1968):1653-1658. D. Barlow, E. Reynolds and S. Agras, "Gender identity change in a transsexual," *Archives of General Psychiatry* 28(1973): 569-576. H. Benjamin, "Clinical Aspects of Transsexualism in Males and Females," *American Journal of Psychotherapy* 11 (1964):458-469. Vern Bullough, "Transsexualism in History," *Archives of Sexual Behavior* 4(1975):561-571, and his *Sexual Variance in Society and History* (Chicago, 1975).

[77]Cook, *op. cit.*, pp. 35, 31. While much of this account is from the *Gilgamesh Epic*, "Eve's" (*Hawwah* in Genesis 3:20 is "mother of all living things" and is a Hebraicized form of the divine name of Heba, Hebat, Khebat, or Khiba, who was the goddess-wife of the Hittite Storm God, combined with Anath (a form of Ishtar) in Hurrian texts; the Greeks called her Hebe, Heracles' goddess-wife) creation from a "rib of Adam" was icontropically taken from the Aliyan account. Uniquely in the original account Adam is portrayed as indescribably beautiful, while Eve seemed like an ape when compared to her divine husband which was far less than the celestial light of the god of creation (see: B. Baba Bathra 58a; Lev. Rab. 20.2). Originally Adam was so tall that the angels mistook him for god; god, being jealous, could not tolerate the challenge and so reduced Adam to 1000

cubits. When he "ate the fruit," thereby angering the god of the park, Adam was reduced to a mere height of one hundred cubits (see:Otzar Midrashim 70f, 238f; Eldad Hadani 66; Hagoren, 40; Sepher Hassidim 200; Gen. Rab. 102, 178; cf. Lev. Rab. 14.1 and 18.2.)

[78]The creation of species is in part from the Egyptian Khnum and/or Ptah, and the Babylonian Arur and/or Ea. As to the substance from which mortals were made, the Greek has *chthon* (earth), the Latin uses *humus*, and Hebrew sites *adama* which was later transliterated into *Adam* (a masculine noun), or Latin *homo*. On the generation of "Adam" see: Sepher Hassidim 290, and Ex. Rab. 40.3. "Eve" is a title—not a sexual distinction, nor was "she" the only "woman" created for "Adam" for Lilith plays a major role in this legend, a woman who went into a rage because Adam demanded that in sex she always lie supine (beneath) him passively while he took the active penetrating role (see: Num. Rab. 16.25). Because Lilith would not accept her "lot" she was "punished" by god and "Adam" was given a second "Eve" who was known as "the First Eve." She, however, was repugnant to Adam, so god "knew he had failed once more" sent her away (Gen. Rab 158, 163-164; Mid. Abkir 133, 135; Abot diR. Nathan 24; B. Sanhedrin 39a) to a place nobody knew. God then made the third Eve who he made beautiful by adorning her with twenty-four pieces of jewelry which "entranced" Adam—out of his tail bone (today's coccyx) (Gen. Rab. 134; B. Erubin 18a—which also suggests that god created the first being androgynous and then later separated the being into man and woman. Philo of Alexandria accepted this account, and argued that the first man (Adam) was bisexual—Philo lived at the same time that Jesus, allegedly, lived).

[79]Cook, *op. cit.*, p. 39. The few ancient cultures that condemned masturbation did so because of their belief that the cosmos was created out of a divine ejaculation ("The Power of the Spurting Seed"). To the Greeks masturbation was not a vice but a "safety-valve," with Greek women using an *olisbos* (dildo) by the third century BCE—a device employed by both heterosexual women and lesbians (see: Herondas, *Two Friends* in *Mimiambus* 6). By the seventh century the Christian church condemned masturbation, giving penances from twenty to forty days to any male over twenty years of age on his first "offense," and one hundred days for a second offense; if the male was so vile as to attempt to masturbate a third (or successive) time, his penance was to be separated from the church and do penance for a year! Masturbation was

considered a "forerunner" to fellatio that if it lead into oral sex the "heathen" would have to do penance for four years. If the "sinner-filled heathen" proceeded to sodomy (anal intercourse) he would have to do penance for seven years! Peter Damiani, an eleventh century clergyman, was so upset about the penance and the act of confession of these sex "crimes against God" that he spoke out against the practice of homosexual offenders making confession to the very men with whom their sins had been committed! (see his *Liber Gomorrhianus* 7). Bishops were given especial jurisdiction to listen to women under 25 years of age detail their masturbation practices, many of which were carefully recorded for "later reflection," as well as the first chance to listen to boys under the age of fourteen detail their homosexual experiences at "great length and in great depth from the time their flushed member [penis] became engorged until it tossed off." No record mentions if the bishop masturbated during this "confession."

[80]Cook, *loc. cit.*

[81]Hooker, *Jonathan Loved David*, pp. 47-58; and my *City of Sodom*. Cf. Genesis 19:4-9a.

[82]Susan Brownmiller, *Against Our Will: Men, Women and Rape* (New York, 1975), pp. 260-261, 272.

[83]See note 81.

[84]*Ibid.*

[85]Ruel L. Howe, *Man's Need and God's Action* (Baltimore, MD, 1953), p. 24.

[86]Bailey, *op. cit.*, pp. 8-21; Horner, *Sex in the Bible*, pp. 58-64, 141-142. Judges 19:22-30 is an excellent demonstration of intent of Old Testament rapists—it was not gender identification or need, but rather an attempt to elevate the group above an individual. The Gibeah story is strictly rape for defilement and is no more sexual than is amputation. See my *Woman in Ancient Israel*.

[87]Cook, *op. cit.*, pp. 47-48, 41, 42, 43, 10; it is a constant sales promotion as is his literature in other pamphlets.

Chapter Three

Cook's Boys

In November of 1983 Colin D. Cook and another man who Homosexual Anonymous literature only lists as "Doug," "a former high school principal," founded Homosexual Anonymous "to pass on to others what they experienced in recovery from homosexuality."[1] According to a letter I received from Mr. Cook, HA by 24 April 1986 had sixty chapters.[2] Convinced that he is "in the service of Christ,"[3] he has lectured in Reading, PA, Daytona Beach, FL, Houston, TX, Rochester, NY, Los Angeles and Boston, and in Indianapolis. A seminar was to be held in Paris on 1-2 November.

Members have been encouraged to send in "faith testimonials" to local newsmedia, and especial-to gay periodicals, magazines, newspapers, weeklies and monthlies. Texas became aware of it no later than 21 March - 28 March 1986,[4] when *This Week In Texas* carried its first notice of the movement. This was followed a week later by an article authored by Carey Jones, who testified that neither the parent body nor any of its members "individually, ...claims to have a "cure."[5] That, at best, is a semantic quibbling, for Cook has argued repeatedly that he is "free" of homosexuality, and was "freed" by Jesus. Semantically "freedom from" and "cure of" are the same.

Jones, in *TWT*, then proceeds to argue that the Bible "clearly place[s] creation in a distinctively heterosexual perspective and further pronounces myriads of blessings on godly heterosexual marriage while simultaneously remaining totally silent on gay relationships." That is only partly correct. The bible is silent on gay relationships. However, it does not place "creation in a distinctively heterosexual perspective." Fundamentalists would note that initial generation of species was "spontaneous creation." Sex, therefore paid no role in beinghood. Rather than a celebration of conjugal bliss, the first "couple" were told that their sexual relationship would be one of pain, enmity, labor and sorrow.[6] Again, if the Old Testament is to be taken literally—a qualification and law commanded and demanded by Homosexuals Anonymous which, like other Christian fundamentalist organizations and clubs, require it to be read as inerrant and without question—Eve did not have Cain and Abel by Adam.[7] Then, after the murder of Abel by Cain Eve had Seth—but by whom? And if he had children who was their mother? Is incest evil? Carey Jones has forgotten that you cannot take one verse literally to prove one point and then to declare other verses to be metaphorical or allegorical so as not to give contradiction to the point just made.

Jone's errors continue in his article. He argues for "specific" bible references and condemns gay courtship and marriage since "There are none [no biblical references to]" but fails to note that while there are no biblical references to gay courtship and marriage, neither are their instructions on heterosexual courtship or marriage (except that "a man is to have but one wife," which most Old Testament men got around anyway). Using the traditionally held but scientifically incorrect assumption that gays are guilty of "fornication...adultery...and promiscuity...activities virtually inseparable from gay experience"[8] he argues that gays must "become the person my Creator and God intends ;... to become"—which he defines as heterosexual.[9] He has forgotten, as Dallas gay historian Phil Johnson was quick to point out, that god did intend some people to be gay[10] since sexual proclivity and orientation is not mentioned in the Christian bible anywhere.

Bastardizing Alfred North Whitehead's discussion on "process of being," Jones argues that this "process" can lead only in one direction—heterosexuality. This argument is given, paradoxically in the same paragraph where he quotes I Corinthians 6:12: "*All* things are lawful to me..." and where he laments "I have no choice over my orientations...." but willingly surrenders any choice he might have had to a god that has made no claims on his orientation.

Jones thesis was quickly taken up by Robert Stephenson of Houston. A man who had had ennumerable difficulties and losses (he lived in terror of his gay orientation the first twenty-five years of his life, then worked actively in several gay organizations and the Metropolitan Community Churches of Omaha and Houston, served prison time for embezzling, lost a lover, became a regular at bars, involved in drugs and generally felt lost to the world) "went back to my Bible." His purpose was to find answers to questions. He was unwilling to assert himself, take a chance, develop his own potentials or self-actualize. Instead Stephenson, like many people today who want a program of their lives spelled out for them, turned to an "authority." Raised a Christian he "turned back to the Bible." Now that he has found comfort in spiritual affairs ("the inner peace") he is "past seeking after pleasures that never really satisfied." In short, Stephenon sublimated his desires by suppressing them for "HA gave me an outlet for the pain and frustration that I could not talk about." Failure to talk about problems only increases their severity and seeming immovability. Avoiding an issue by turning to another one only postpones the inevitable which will require greater strength, resolve, and fortitude to overcome.[11] A truly self-actualized individual accepts his or herself for what he/she is: a homosexual who accepts her/his condition and adapts to it in a way that she/he is comfortable. As David H. pointed out, "The homosexual who denies his sexuality might join a group such as "Homosexuals Anonymous," denying his condition or feeling he has been "cured."[12] But *feeling* "cured" and *being* "cured" are quite different. The former is euphoric fantasy, while the latter is actuality.[13]

The same inability to accept the plethora of emotions coupled with sexual orientation—be it heterosexual or homosexual—which frequently leads to a malaise of thinking, self-condemnation and personal mental abuse,[14] appeared in a letter submitted to *TWT*[15] the last week of April 1986. The writer cried that "I had experienced, as have *many* others, the low points of homosexuality. I had been used, abused, misused and confused." The writer did not stop at this point, reflect that *many* heterosexuals also feel "used, abused, misused, and confused," and still carry on their lives without changing to homosexuality, but instead issued a hyperhebraic horatory lamentation and then turned to Homosexuals Anonymous, found Jesus, "And guess what? Voila! I was straight [heterosexual].... it is not too difficult to be free from that junk [homosexuality] once you give it to the Lord[16]...]

The controversy surrounding these letters, inspired David Hawkins, also from Houston, to write to *TWT*. Hawkins argues, "Once a man's mind is free from *religion*, he has a *far, far* better chance for a happy life."[17] The real problem is confessiological organized fundamental religion limiting the development of the individual psychologically, socially, sexually and ethically has done great harm not only to the individual, but to the society in which the individual lives, works, and dialogues verbally or in writing. Much of this fundamental movement is the result of political posturing of religion which has as its ultimate aim the control of society, the enrichment of its clergy at the expense of its congregations, and the transmorgification of freedom into a theocratic despotism.[18]

The great homophobe, Charles Stanley, one-time President of the Southern Baptist Convention, has had the unique distinction of claiming that AIDS and other diseases are the judgment of god upon gay people. William E. Swing, Episcopal Bishop of California was among the few Christian clergymen who would stand up for human rights and denounce the SBC President, condemning his homophobia and detailing that rather than it being "God" who was smiting gays, it was "the wrath of the moral community leaders throughout this land!" who disguised themselves as being servants of god. [19]

The few clergymen who do argue for the rights of gay people either qualify their approval by claiming that "The homosexual is generally not responsible for his [sic] condition" and acknowledges that "Celibacy and sublimation are not always possible or even desirable for the homosexual. There are many somewhat [sic!] stable homosexual unions which afford their partners some human fulfillment and contentment."[20] This affectatiousness is tantamount to patting the homosexual on the head and then labeling the homosexual to be a "leper."[21] Their knowledge of the bible is limited to their training, preconditioning and own psychology concerning homosexuality.

What few ministers of the Christian and Jewish faith realize is that the primary message in the Old Testament concerning sexual morality is love which must be coupled with a respect for the other person regardless of gender of either party, when "sin" invades sexual love it comes when one person dishonors the other person as a fellow human being by using that person as a chattle to pleasure themself, with orgasm/ejaculation being the purpose rather than the result of the interaction.[22]

Marriage does not play the same role in the Old Testament as it does in the New Testament. The Old Testament marriage was a connection between god and people; marriage in the New Testament is a joining of two people into one—there is no gender qualification and thus is applicable to heterosexuals as well as gays. Furthermore, whereas marriage in the Old Testament is an obligatory connection between deity and damned, marriage in the New Testament is a personal loving tie between two equals—it is their love which is to be "fertile"—not their bodies.[23] This is the graphic reality of Acts 8:26-39, where the eunuch, who had been denied access to the Old Testament community since "[he] had his testicles crushed or his penis cut off" (cf. Deut. 23:1), was admitted to the New Testament community. This is symbolic that those who do not marry or bear children are as acceptable to god as those who do marry and bear children—including gay people!

Where the Roman Catholic church and other fundamentalist Christian churches have argued that "The procreative aspect becomes the primary and sometimes the only purpose of sexuality,"[24] they reject their own teachings which allegedly are buttressed by tradition.[25] Sexual love involves the good of the whole person,[26] not just the chance meeting of sperm with ova, or the emission of seminal fluids. To argue that woman's "exclusive function" is to bear children depersonalizes her into a baby-factory,* while to declare that a man's function is to "produce" seed for babies makes him a pharmacy. Humankind was never called to function according to biological givens, but rather to interact in a loving and caring relationship regardless of gender. For a man to use a wife as a convenient masturbatory instrument is as wrong as it is for a woman to use a man's penis for clitorial stimulation or precreation: love, the message of the New Testament, is degraded and animalistic coupling substituted.

When love between two individuals is enthroned, and "procreation" relegated to the place it belongs as a possible result of love and not the reason for love, "promiscuity" alleged in homosexuality, and on the rise in heterosexuality, will decline. Such a thesis would have helped Colin Cook before his own downfall, and the tragedy of self-deception became the *raison d'etre* of his coterie.

---

*Cf. Rosemary Radford Ruether, *Liberation Theology* (New York: Paulist Press, 1972), p. 105.

The issue of homosexuality has been centered around sexuality—not love. This became especially graphic when Dr. Ron Lawson, a sociology professor at Queens College in New York and Seventh Day Adventist Kinship (a "gay men and women and their friends" organization) released a thirteen page letter detailing the results of interviews with 14 Quest participants.[27]

Colin Cook's diatribes and lamentations on and against homosexuality were fantasy at best and blatant hypocrisy at worse. He used his organization, Homosexuals Anonymous, and the Quest Center to have same-sex encounters with the very men he allegedy was helping "to become free" of their homosexuality.

On 3 November 1986, Cook released a letter in response to the findings of Dr. Lawson. In it he admitted that he had engaged in "hugs to erection" and "semi-nude/nude massages" with males who went to Quest in hopes of being "cured" or "made free" of their homosexuality. He excused his actions on the grounds that he "deluded" himself to believe that the semi-nude/nude massages and "hugs to erection" were "simply nurturing or desensitizing that had got out of control." He admitted "In this I now see I was rationalizing. I was really involved in seduction."[28]

The "counselees" added more details. Angry and confused, most felt that they had been sexually abused by Cook—manipulated for his own gratification. Eleven of the fourteen interviewed detailed the erotic hugs "to erection," while nine of the fourteen complained that Cook insisted on repeatedly going over the details of their sexual fantasies and experiences "titillating himself at their expense." Twelve of the fourteen reported that Cook had urged them to undergo nude massages with him.[29]

Dan Robert, the HAFS Service Coordinator, presented further details. Cook invited his counselees to engage in "mutual masturbation."[30] Yet at the same time, Roberts argued for the continuation of HA and HAFS, asking the members for their prayers and continued support while HA and Quest reorganize (which is to include changing address and telephone number) since "Our common welfare should come first, personal recovery depends on HA unity." He plays the usual "god-message," excusing Cook, claiming "sexual falls are desires for power, domination and glory," while "True brotherhood—and sisterhood—along with harmony and love, fortified by clear insights and right practices, are the only answers."[31]

Roberts could not admit that the Seventh Day Adventist contribution of over $47,000 a year to HAFS/Quest[32] played any role in his decision to continue the discredited organization. The proclaimed solidarity with Exodus International, an "other 'ex-gay' ministr[y]'" and similar organizations,[33] was to become the shrevement, the pardon, the alkahest to soothe the wound Cook inflicted by fondling the men he had promised to "lead out" of the darkness of homosexuality into a pristine purity of heterosexuality that he proclaimed on lecture circuits he shared and enjoyed with his wife and two sons.

What Roberts did not address was the one good that Cook did perform: he did much to lead the Seventh Day Adventist Church into an awareness of its thousands of gay and lesbian members. Not only does the Cook scandal expose the lie of there being a "Christian cure" for homosexuality, it unwillingly addresses the reality that there are thousands of good gay men and lesbians who are vital and contributing forces to the church, society, and humankind.[34]

Among the facts Roberts and other homophobes in the Seventh Day Adventist Church have overlooked is that none of the "counselees" at Quest changed his sexual orientation—and no one knew of anyone who had. All those interviewed by Lawson argue that Cook "has not been cured," and doubted their own "curability"—a phenomenon that is impossible given the human psyche.[35]

Another positive that has come out of this situation is that gay Seventh Day Adventists who had turned to Cook and Quest have come to more easily accept their own homosexuality. Not only is it now easier to accept their essential gaity and gayness, but they have "learned to abide in Jesus"—they are comfortable with themselves and their learned ontology and religious confessiology.[36]

The greatest negative to come out of the Cook confidence-game against Christian fundamental gays, as well as gay Christians who are not fundamentalists or religious primitives, is Cook's lack of professionalism and void of psychological reality[37] which has cost gay men and women who might seek services of a psychologist or psychiatrist for matters other than their own sexual orientation, are, to varying degrees, sceptical if not hostile, to the entire profession.

Colin Cook left a legacy of self-hatred. Condemning homosexuality as being promiscuous and "compulsive behavior"—based on his own personal experiences,[38] he has given additional fuel to the verbal and physically discriminatory and abusive fires of other homophobes who mascarade as charitable and/or religious figures.[39] Thus Raoul Dederen, professor of historical theology at Andrews University Theological Seminary, Berrien Springs, Michigan, continues the same line of thinking that homosexuality is somehow unbiblical and "evil." He condemns theological writings that accept homosexuality,[40] and joyfully proceeds to distort the original texts of Old and New Testaments.

Introducing I Timothy 1:10, and other New Testament "condemnations" of homosexuality, Dederen argues for "a simple reading of the context," which, for him, must be taken literally (with the unique comment on Romans 1:24-27, that *all* human sexuality, whether heterosexual or homosexual, is depicted as disordered by man's inherent drive toward self-centeredness, his rebellion against God, and the chaos that the Fall provoked." In light of the present evidence, it seems valid to conclude that Romans 1:26, 27 understands homosexual practice to be sin in and of itself." Yet Dederen forgets that just prior to this final comment, he argued that it includes *all* human sexuality (emphasis his), and not solely homosexuality.).

Dederen's arguments against homosexuality as being condemned by other biblical verses does not hold any moreso than his initial claim. He cites Genesis 2:24, and refers to Mark 10:48, as proof that god created a "relationship between male and female." [41] But Genesis 2:24 does *not* make such a claim literally, allegorically, or figuratively. The line merely states that "they [plural in number] become one flesh." Originally this line was a testimony to the matriarchal custom in Palestine, and is an argument for a common characteristic of people—a sense of commonwealth, community identity, familial—in the broadest sense—orientation. In fact, the verse means for a man to go to the home of the subordinate (wife) as a statement of matriarchal binding. [42] To couple this ancient Cretanopalestinic line with Mark 10:48 is absurd. They have no relation.

Dederen's comment that "the testimony of Jesus and Paul about Creation, marriage, and the Fall, are parts of a whole fabric that unanimously and undeviatingly portrays heterosexual love as God's will, and therefore as good and normative" cannot be sustained or substantiated by scripture. Jesus made no claims for or against any aspect, condition, orientation or expression of sexuality. His references to love are all gender-free. As for Saul (Paul), his primary interest was in a sexless society. [43]

The "cases of men who claim to have changed their sexual orientation from exclusive homosexuality through participation in a pentacostal church fellowship,"[44] is obnoxious. The men were not "cured" but given psychological reasons (good or bad is irrelevant) to adopt a heterosexual orientation and heterosexual expression—as did Colin Cook. How long their "cure" lasts is not yet known; Cook's "cure" obviously never took place—in spite of Cook's comment "Where sin increased, grace increased all the more."[45]

NOTES

[1] "Homosexuality and the Church," *loc. cit.*

[2] Dated 24 April 1986.

[3] *Ibid.*

[4] Carey Jones, "Homosexuals Anonymous: Being Heterosexual Is Not the Issue," *This Week In Texas* 12(2, 28 March - 3 April 1986):26-27.

[5] *Ibid.*, p. 26.Cf. "Homosexuality and the Church," p. [2].

[6] Genesis 3:15-16.

[7] Cf. Hagadol Gen. 88-89, 105. Cp. Tosephta Sota 5:17 and 18; Abot diR. Nathan 1:7-8; Gen. Rab. 168-169, 171-172; ancient records state that YHWH was the father of Cain, see: *Vita Adea* 18-21; *Apoc. of Moses* 1. The name "Cain" means "stalk" (*gayin* from *qganiti* which was later *qaneh*) and therefore is allegorical about a farmer.

[8] Legend has the daughters of Cain seducing the sons of Seth, and thereby developing the forces of good and evil. The only records we have on the birth of Seth come in later Talmudic accounts. It is said that Adam, fearing another Abel, abstained from sex with his wife for 130 years, during which time he experienced the "sin" of involuntary emissions "of seed." See: Tanhuma Buber Gen. 20; Gen. Rab. 195-196, 204, 225-226, 236; B. Erubin 18b; Pesiqta Rabbati, 67b. Seth was originally a consolation (the meaning of the name Seth); see:

Adamschriften 36.

[9]Jones, *loc. cit..* Cook, *Homosexuality: An Open Door?*, p. 30f.

[10]Phil Johnson, "HA: Deja Vu," *This Week In Texas* 12(5, 18-24 April 1986):21-22.

[11]Robert Stephenson, "Out of Gay Life thru HA," *This Week In Texas* 12(3, 4-10 April 1986):23.

[12]David H., "Homosexuals Anonymous...Gamblers Anonymous...Overeaters Anonymous and Alcoholic Anonymous," *This Week In Texas* 11(52, 14-20 March 1986):23.

[13]John R. Cavanagh, "The Psychotherapy of Homosexuality, 1. Some Thoughts on Individual Therapy," *Psychiatric Opinion* 4(2, 1967):4-8, argues that "cures" for homosexuality is more possible among those gays who desire to have children (with lesbians being more prone to seek "curing" than are gay males), but is more "successful" when therapy includes electrical shock treatment—the thesis of D.F. Clark, "A Note on Avoidance Conditioning Techniques in Sexual Disorder," *Behavior Research and Therapy* 3(3, 1965):203-206, a more sophisticated form of Pavlovian conditioning. Yet Russell R. Monroe and Morton L. Enelow, "The Therapeutic Motivation in Male Homosexuals: An Adaptational Analysis," *American Journal of Psychotherapy* 14(3, 1960):474-490, notes that homosexuals who are coerced into treatment do not respond to the treatment. O. Spurgeon English, "A Primer on Homosexuality," *GP [General Practice]* 7(4, 1953):55-60 notes that "cures" for homosexuality is impossible. Cp. Rene Guyon "The Causes of Homosexuality: A Symposium," *Sexology* 21 (11, 1955):722f.

[14]Donald Webster Cory and John P. LeRoy, "Why Homosexuals Resist Cure," *Sexology* 30(7, 1964):480-482. Bills, *loc. cit..* Eugene A. Kaplan, "Homosexuality: A Search for the Ego-Ideal," *Archives of General Psychiatry* 16(3, 1967):355-358. An essay on the naturalness of homosexuality in relationship to heterosexuality and sexual response is in Eckhard H. Hess, Allan L. Seltzer and John M. Shlien, "Pupil Response of Hetero- and Homo-sexual Males to Pictures of Men and Women: A Pilot Study," *Journal of Abnormal and Social Psychology* 70(3, 1965):165-168. See also Ruth Marjorie McGuire, "An Inquiry into Attitudes and Value Systems of a Minority Group: A Comparative Study of Attitudes and

Values Systems of Adult Male Homosexuals with Adult Male Heterosexuals," Ph.D. dissertation, New York University, 1960, 180 pp.

[15] *This Week In Texas* hereafter abbreviated to *TWT.* Scholars, unfortunately, ignore popular gay news media. This is regretable inasmuch as most serious gay news media is not only well written, as is the case with *TWT,* but frequently is in the forefront of news concerning gays and people sympathetic to supportive of gays and gay rights.

[16]"HA: Not to Bore," *TWT* 12(6, 25 April - 1 May 1986):21.

[17]David M. Hawkins, "HA & Religion," *TWT* 12(4, 11-17 April 1986):19. Cp. *ibid.*, pp. 19-21.

[18]Cf. my *Evangelical Terrorism: Censorship, Falwell, Robertson & the Seamy Side of Christian Fundamentalism,* (Irving, TX, 1986).

[19]William E. Swing, "HA & the Bible," *TWT* 12(3, 4-10 April 1986):22-23. See bibliography below, p. 76.

[20]Charles Curran, *Catholic Moral Theology in Dialogue* (Notre Dame, IN, 1969), p. 217.

[21]Joseph Epstein, "Homo/Hetero: The Struggle for Sexual Identity," *Harper's* (September 1970).

[22]Cf. T.C. DeKruijf, *The Bible on Sexuality* (DePere, WI, 1966), p. 53.

[23]*Ibid.*, pp. 67-69.

[24]Curran, *op. cit.*, p. 199.

[25]Pius XI, *Casti Connubii* (No. 59) in *Seven Great Encyclicals* (Paramus, NJ, 1963), pp. 93-94.

[26]See note 8, above. Cf. John J. McNeill, *The Church and the Homosexual* (New York, 1985). 211 pp.

[27]"Colin Cook Resigns as Director of Quest Learning Center," *SDA Kinship Connection* 10(11, December, 1986), p. 1. This material comes as courtesy of Jere Hinckley of Dallas.

70

[28]Colin Cook, "Colin Cook Writes," *SDA Kinship Connection* (February 1987), p. 8.

[29]"The Shakeup: Ron Lawson's Letter of October 23, 1986," *SDA Kinship Connection* (February 1987):3-6, note especially page 4. Colin agonizes, "Where I have nakedly massaged a counselee, where I have done that to him, I have sinned, done wrong..." Many of those who went to Cook at Quest in Reading, Pennsylvania, did so because of his publicity and his appearance with his wife on television, and/or because they had heard about his children. Others read "success stories ... in church periodicals. Counselors at Adventist schools have told students about Colin's "deliverance from homosexuality." Colin [became]... a symbol of hope." *Ibid.*, p. 4.

[30]Dan Roberts (his name is spelled both Roberts and Robert's in the *Kinship Connection*), "Resignation of Colin Cook as director of Quest Learning Center," *SDA Kinship Connection* (January 1987):7.

[31]*Ibid.*, p. 8.

[32]*Ibid..*

[33]*Ibid.* Cf. *The Exodus Standard* 3(1, 1986). Meri Bradley of Houston, Texas, is a counselor with a M.Ed. in guidance and counseling from the University of Houston, and uses "the Gospel of Jesus Christ" as her psychological text book (*ibid*, p. 3), and, like the majority of the people who operate the organization are heterosexual homophobes who come from a strict Christian fundamentalist background, many of whom are parents who are pledged to keep their children from the "darkness" of homosexuality. The sad part of their "ministry" is that they treat with theological terror those whom they fear have fallen "prey" to homosexuality They applaud "Family Matters" (*ibid.*, p. 9) as if pregnancy (and especially regular pregnancy) will deter or end homosexuality. Their insistance on the literal interpretation of the Judaeo-Christian bible can be seen in Darlene Bogle's "God Set Me Free from Lesbianism," *Christian Family Magazine* (1984). Among its members are "Episcopalians for Biblical Sexuality" a unique distortion of biblical accounts on sex. See my *Sex, Pornography and the Bible*, with Ronald Wayne Hurt, forthcoming.

[34]Lawson, *op. cit.*, (January 1987), p. 6.

71

[35] *Ibid.*, p. 4.

[36] *Ibid.*

[37] *Ibid.*, pp. 4-5.

[38] *Ibid*, p. 5. Cf. Cook, *Homosexuality: An Open Door?*, pp. 12, 24, 35-36; cp. his tape, *Homosexuality and the Power to Change.*

[39] Cf. *Exodus Standard.*

[40] Raoul Dederen, "Homosexuality: A Biblical Perspective," *Ministry* (September, 1981), reprinted in "The H Solution," *loc. cit.*, pp. [12-14].

[41] *Ibid.*, p. 13.

[42] Robert Graves and Raphael Patai, *The Hebrew Myths: The Book of Genesis* (New York, 1964; reprint, 1966), p. 13. Cf. Robert Graves, *The White Goddess: A Historical Grammar of Poetic Myth* (New York, 1948; revised, 1966), pp. 226, 316.

[43] Sidney Tarachow, "St. Paul and Early Christianity: A Psychoanalytic and Historical Study," *Psychoanalysis and the Social Sciences*, ed. W. Muensterberger, 4 (1955):232. Saul (Paul) may have been a latent homosexual; see: *ibid.*, p. 270. Saul's opposition to sex is found in I Corinthians 7:1-8, 9, where he condemns remarriage, sexual heterosexual passion, and encourages total abstinence (I Corinthians 7:25-29).

[44] E. Mansell Pattison and Myrna Loy Pattison, "Ex-Gays,' Religious Mediated Change in Homosexuals," *American Journal of Psychiatry* 137(12, December 1980):1553-1563. Dederen also cites Robert K. Johnston, "Homosexuality: (1) Can It Be 'Cured'?" *The Reformed Journal* (March 1981): 11-12. Sublimation and substitution, like Pavlovian conditioning is an old technique, see: John R. Ernst, "Homosexuality and Crime," *Journal of Clinical Psychopathology* 8(5, 1947): 763-769; and, Mark Tarail, "New Treatments for the Homosexual," 1961, reprinted in *The Third Sex*, ed. Isadore Rubin, *op. cit.*, pp. 63-66, who recommended "changing" (curing) a homosexual by means of "reconditioning therapy ["brainwashing"], physical and environmental withdrawal [coercion] (and) psychotherapy and motivation therapy [Pavlovian con-

72

ditioning." Interestingly, as early as 1947, studies were released showing that "treatment" of homosexuals had a marginal success rate, see: F.H. Taylor, "Homosexual Offenders and Their Relation to Psychotherapy," *British Medical Journal* (4526, 1947):525-529; cp. "Treatment of Homosexuality," *British Medical Journal* (4442, 1946):300, (5083, 1958):1347.

Organized fundamental religion has had a negative effect on gays who have become victimized by religious zealots. See, James Herman VanderVelt and Robert P. Odenwald, *Psychiatry and Catholicism* (2d ed., New York, 1957) 474 pp., Winifred M. Whiteley and C.H. Whitely, "Unfruitful Sex," in their *Sex & Morals* (New York, 1967), pp. 79-100; and Robert Watson Wood, *Christ and the Homosexual: Some Observations* (New York, 1962) 221, arguing that Christ taught against homosexuality (he didn't). His work, and that by Helmut Thielicke (*The Ethics of Sex*), and H. Kimball Jones (*Toward a Christian Understanding of Homosexuality*) are analyzed in "Three Studies of Homosexuality in Relation to the Christian Faith," by Daniel Day Williams, *Social Action* 34(4, 1967):30-37. Williams concludes that the church has much to learn about homosexuality and the perspective of the Christian faith upon this normal aspect of human life and sexual exchange.

[45]*SDA Kinship Connection* (February 1987):8. Those who participated in Quest's "cure program" did not feel the same way. "Charles Arthur" [pseudonym] was told that nude massages were "part of the program" and participating in them "was supposed to help" cure him (he has now accepted himself as a gay Christian). When he did not show "progress" in overcoming his homosexuality he was "blamed for not making 'progress,' and so I carried that guilt"—a classic case of transference. *Ibid.*, p. 5. Jym Stuart (*ibid.*, p. 6) noted that "Colin Cook was not 'cured' or 'delivered' from his homosexuality," and writes that while Cook is now out, Homosexuals Anonymous Fellowship Services "is still being supported and pushed as the program for 'delivering' homosexuals—using the very same materials that Colin helped to develop!" He adds "To liken homosexuality to alcoholism and tell gay people that their lot in life is to stay sober (abstain from sex under all conditions, unless of course they get married to a person of the opposite sex) is, in my opinion, a crime against nature. This "sobriety" is a cross no one should have to bear."

73

INDICES

ABOUT THE AUTHOR

Iowa born and initially educated in Iowa (State College of Iowa and University of Northern Iowa), Arthur Frederick Ide is the author of more than 200 published books. His works include, most recently, *City of Sodom & Homosexuality in Western Religious Thought to 630 CE* (Monument Press), *Gomorrah & the Rise of Homophobia* (The Liberal Press), *Loving Women: A Study of Lesbianism to 500 CE* (Liberal Arts), and *Evangelical Terrorism: Censorship, Falwell, Robertson & the Seamy Side of Christian Fundamentalism* (Scholars Books), as well as various psychoanalytic works, such as *Martyrdom of Women: A Study of Death Psychology in the Early Christian Church to 301 CE* (Tangelwuld), and *Calendar of Death: Socio-Psychological Factors in Thomas of Canterbury's Attitude Toward His Own Death* (Scholars).

Fluent in Arabic, Latin, Greek and other Old Testament languages, he has published numerous books on the teachings of Jesus and the Early Church Fathers, as well as the role of sex in religion. Graduate degrees include theology, psychology and socio-history. Dr. Ide took his last degree from Carnegie-Mellon University, and has taught in all fields at various institutions of higher learning—including church history at the University of San Diego and Mauna Olu College of Hawaii (where he also taught philosophy) Ide now lectures nationally on Christian Fundamentalism and democracy.

Ide is a member of People for the American Way, Planned Parenthood, American Civil Liberties Union, National Organization for Women, Fundamentalists Anonymous, and numerous other civil rights organizations.

Suggested Additional Reading

Bayer, Ronald. *Homosexuality and American Psychiatry: the Politics of Diagnosis* (New York: Basic Books, 1981).

Clark, J. Michael, "AIDS, Death, and God: Gay Liberational Theology and the Problem of Suffering." *Journal of Pastoral Counseling* 21.1(1968):40-54.

Clark, J. Michael. *Gay Being: Divine Presence: Essays in Gay Spirituality (The Ganymede Papers)* (Garland: Tangelwuld Press, 1987).

DeCecco, John P. *Bashers, Baiters & Bigots: Homophobia in America* (New York: Harrington Park Press, 1984).

Fisher, Peter. *The Gay Mystique: The Myth and Reality of Homosexuality* (New York: Stein and Day, 1979).

Fortunato, John E. "AIDS: The Plague That Lays Waste at Noon." *The Witness* 68.9(September 1985):6-9.

Gonsiorek, John. *Homosexuality and Psychotherapy* (New York: The Haworth Press, 1981)

Hancock, L. "Fear and Healing in the AIDS Crisis." *Christianity and Crisis* (24 June 1985):255-258.

Howell, L. "Churches and AIDS: Responsibilities in Mission." *Christianity and Crisis* (9 December 1985):483-484.

Ide, Arthur Frederick. *City of Sodom & Homosexuality in Western Religious Thought to 600 CE.* (Dallas: Monument Press, 1984).

Ide, Arthur Frederick. *Gomorrah and the Rise of Homophobia* (Las Colinas: The Liberal Press, 1985).

Ide, Arthur Frederick. *Loving Women: A Study of Lesbianism to 500 CE* (Arlington: Liberal Arts Press, 1985).

Johnston, Maury. *Gays Under Grace: A Gay Christian's Response to the Moral Majority* (Nashville: Winston-Derek Publishers, 1983).

Koertge, Noretta (Gen. Ed.). *Nature and Causes of Homosexuality: A Philosophic and Scientific Inquiry* (New York: The Haworth Press, 1981).

Licata, Sal and Robert Petersen. *Historical Perspectives on Homosexuality* (New York: The Haworth Press, 1980).

Nelson, James B. "Responding to, Learning from AIDS." *Christianity and Crisis* (19 May 1986):176-181.

Ross, Michael W. *Homosexuality, Masculinity and Femininity.* (New York: Harrington Park Press, 1984).

Schoenberg, Robert and Richard Goldberg with David A. Shore. *With Compassion Toward Some: Homosexuality and Social Work in America* (New York: Harrington Park Press, 1983).

Weinberg, George. *Society and the Healthy Homosexual.* (New York: St. Martin's Press, 1972).